Communication – A 30-Day Mindset Transformation Guide

Daily Lessons to Reframe Communication as a Leadership Discipline, Not a Soft Skill

Andy Page, Ph.D.

Published by EBR Technologies

Communication – A 30-Day Mindsets Transformation Guide

Copyright © 2025 EBR Technologies

All rights reserved. No part of this book may be reproduced, stored in a retrieval system, or transmitted in any form or by any means—electronic, mechanical, photocopying, recording, or otherwise—without prior written permission of the publisher.

ISBN: 979-8-9939275-8-9

Printed in the United States of America
Published by EBR Technologies

Communication – A 30-Day Mindset Transformation Guide

Daily Lessons to Reframe Communication as a Leadership Discipline, Not a Soft Skill

Part of the *30-Day Mindset Transformation Series*

Other Books in the 30-Day Mindset Transformation Series

Reliability – A 30-Day Mindset Transformation Guide
Daily Lessons in Evidence-Based Thinking to Create a Reliability Mindset

---

Change & Culture – A 30-Day Mindset Transformation Guide
Daily Lessons Using the R3/R4 Change Model™ to Create a Shift in the Culture of Your Organization

---

Safety & Risk – A 30-Day Mindset Transformation Guide
Daily Lessons In Evidence-Based Safety: Merging Human Leadership and System Discipline

---

Problem-Solving – A 30-Day Mindset Transformation Guide
Daily Lessons in How to See Problems Differently and Develop More Effective Solutions

---

Sustainable Performance – A 30-Day Mindset Transformation Guide
Daily Lessons to Engineer Consistency, Prevent Burnout, and Sustain Results That Matter

---

Abstract Thinking – A 30-Day Mindset Transformation Guide
Daily Lessons for Consuming and Translating Abstract Concepts into Actionable Meaning

Communication – A 30-Day Mindsets Transformation Guide

Disclaimer

This book is intended for educational and professional development purposes. The concepts, methods, and examples presented reflect the author's experience and interpretation of best practices within the fields of maintenance, reliability, and organizational culture.

While every effort has been made to ensure accuracy and clarity, the information provided is not a substitute for sound engineering judgment, professional advice, or site-specific analysis. Readers are encouraged to adapt these ideas to their own organizations responsibly, with appropriate technical validation and safety consideration.

Neither the author nor EBR Technologies, LLC assumes any responsibility for outcomes resulting from the application of the material in this book. All implementation decisions remain the sole responsibility of the reader and their organization.

Names and examples of companies, individuals, and situations have been used for illustrative purposes only and do not represent actual entities or events unless explicitly stated.

Communication – A 30-Day Mindsets Transformation Guide

Table of Contents

Dedication 1
Abstract 2
Author's Note 3
Foreword 4
How to Use This 30-Day Guide 6
Why the Emphasis on Mindsets? 8
THE EBR COMMUNICATION FRAMEWORK 10
DAY 1 — The Sender Owns the Burden of Communication 16
DAY 2 — Communication Is the Transfer of Meaning, Not the Delivery of Words 18
DAY 3 — Assumptions Are the Silent Killers of Communication 20
DAY 4 — Speak in the Receiver's Terms 22
DAY 5 — The Difference Between Information and Meaning 24
DAY 6 — Evidence as the Stabilizer of Meaning 26
DAY 7 — Context Is Never Complete Without Evidence 28
DAY 8 — Reducing Noise by Using Observables 30
DAY 9 — Signal vs. Story 32
DAY 10 — Evidence Before Urgency 34
DAY 11 — Interpretation Is the Failure Point 36
DAY 12 — Meaning-Making as a Leadership Skill 38
DAY 13 — Designing Messages for Human Filters 40
DAY 14 — The Receiver Cannot Detect Their Own Misunderstanding 42
DAY 15 — "Tell Me How You're Interpreting This" 44

Communication – A 30-Day Mindsets Transformation Guide

DAY 16 — The EBR Communication Structure 46
DAY 17 — Why Every Message Must End with Action 48
DAY 18 — Implications: Thinking Downstream............................ 50
DAY 19 — Coordination Instead of Compliance............................ 52
DAY 20 — Preventing Isolation in Communication........................ 54
DAY 21 — Drift: Communication's Silent Failure Mode 56
DAY 22 — The Drift Check as a Leadership Habit........................ 58
DAY 23 — The Cost of Unchecked Drift 60
DAY 24 — Resetting Alignment After Drift 62
DAY 25 — Cadence as a Control System 64
DAY 26 — Communication as a Reliability Process........................ 66
DAY 27 — Proportional Communication 68
DAY 28 — Communication as Collaboration.................................. 70
DAY 29 — Surfacing Unintended Consequences Early 72
DAY 30 — The Complete EBR Alignment Loop............................. 74
BONUS DAY — Communication as a Leadership Identity 76
The 10 Communication Failure Modes (and Their Countermeasures) 78
The EBR Communication Scripts for Tough Moments 82
The Proportional Communication Map 88
The EBR Communication Audit Tool 92
The EBR Conversation Builder Template 96
Closing Reflections.. 102
About the Author 104
About EBR Technologies 105
Author's Note on the Use of AI 106

Communication – A 30-Day Mindsets Transformation Guide

♦

♦

Dedication

To the people who taught me that communication is not noise, volume, or persuasion —
but the quiet discipline of helping others see clearly.

To every leader who has ever paused long enough to explain the "why,"
who chose patience over pressure,
who took responsibility for being understood instead of blaming others for misunderstanding.

To the teams who keep showing up,
doing the work,
asking the questions they were never given enough context to answer —
your persistence is the reason clarity matters.

And to my own family, who remind me every day
that the most important conversations are never about performance,
but about connection, understanding, and the courage to speak with honesty and care.

This book is for all of you —
for anyone who believes that clarity is kindness,
that understanding is leadership,
and that communication, done well,
can change not just outcomes,
but people.

Abstract

Effective communication is not an interpersonal preference or a leadership style—it is a skill that can be improved...to an expert level if you want. Misunderstandings, delays, rework, and conflict rarely originate from technical issues; they originate from gaps in clarity, context, and interpretation. This book presents a structured, evidence-based approach to communication built on the premise that **the sender carries the responsibility for the accuracy, alignment, and reliability of understanding.**

Across thirty days of focused lessons, the book reframes communication as the transfer of meaning through an engineered sequence: beginning with observable evidence, shaping the correct interpretation, clarifying implications, and directing required action. Each lesson reveals where communication typically breaks down and provides a disciplined framework for preventing drift, ambiguity, and assumption. The model emphasizes early communication, proportional information flow, verification of comprehension, and the design of messages that anticipate human filters, cognitive biases, and operational pressures.

By integrating principles from reliability engineering, behavioral psychology, and practical leadership, this book offers a repeatable system that helps leaders build clarity into their processes and relationships. The outcome is communication that reduces uncertainty, strengthens trust, accelerates alignment, and enables teams to act with confidence and precision.

Communication – A 30-Day Mindsets Transformation Guide

Author's Note

Communication has always been treated as a soft skill, an interpersonal preference, or a personality trait. But after decades in plants, conference rooms, control rooms, and executive offices, I've learned something different: most problems do not begin as technical failures—they begin as communication failures. Misalignment, drift, assumption, silence, vague direction, and late updates cost more than any broken component ever could.

This book was written because I've watched too many good people struggle—not from lack of effort, but from lack of clarity. They were asked to execute without understanding. They were handed responsibility without context. They were left to interpret meaning without evidence. And they carried the consequences of misunderstandings they never caused.

The EBR Communication Framework exists to fix that. It reframes communication as a workflow process, not a personality-driven talent. When understanding becomes something you **engineer**, not something you **hope for**, everything changes: decisions improve, timelines stabilize, people trust each other more, and the work becomes lighter instead of heavier.

My hope is that these pages give you more than techniques—they give you a way of thinking. A way of approaching conversations with intention. A way of reducing uncertainty for the people who depend on you. A way of taking responsibility for clarity so that others can do their best work without guessing.

If this book helps make one conversation cleaner, one update sooner, one expectation clearer, or one relationship stronger, then it has already done its job.

Thank you for giving these ideas space in your life and leadership.

— Andy Page, Ph.D.
Founder, EBR Technologies

Communication — A 30-Day Mindsets Transformation Guide

Foreword

Every organization believes it communicates well.
Most discover — usually too late — that they do not.

The gap between what was said and what was understood is where projects unravel, relationships strain, schedules slip, and trust erodes. It is in this gap that drift begins: the kind of slow, quiet misalignment that eventually becomes conflict, delay, or failure. And in the modern workplace, where complexity increases faster than clarity, communication has become the most underestimated operational risk leaders face.

What you will find in this book is not another collection of tips, slogans, or clever phrases. It is a **framework** — a disciplined, evidence-based approach to communication that treats understanding as an engineered outcome, not an accidental one. This book reframes communication as a reliability function: something that must be designed, sequenced, verified, and maintained with the same rigor we apply to our equipment, our processes, and our decisions.

This book teaches a principle many leaders acknowledge but few practice: **the sender carries the responsibility for clarity.**
Not the listener. Not the team. Not the circumstance.
The sender.

Through thirty days of precise, actionable lessons, Andy shows that communication is not simply what is spoken — it is what is constructed in the mind of another person. And because interpretation is shaped by fatigue, pressure, incentives, emotion, and history, leaders cannot rely on hope or good intention. They must build messages that anticipate human filters, eliminate ambiguity, and validate comprehension before action begins.

Communication – A 30-Day Mindsets Transformation Guide

What makes this work different is its combination of humanity and structure. This book attempts to reflect the grounded realism of someone who has spent decades in the field — in manufacturing facilities, maintenance shops, leadership rooms, and project war rooms where a single misunderstanding can cost time, money, or safety. Yet also honoring the empathy of those who understand that communication is deeply human: emotional, psychological, and context-dependent.

The result is a book that is both **technical** and **personal**, both **practical** and **transformational**. It gives leaders a way to strengthen not only their messages, but their relationships, their credibility, and their culture.

If you read these pages slowly — one lesson at a time — you will begin to see patterns you never noticed, assumptions you never questioned, and habits you never examined. You will catch misalignment earlier. You will send cleaner messages. You will confirm understanding instead of inferring it. And the people around you will feel the difference long before you realize you've changed.

This book will not simply make you a better communicator.
It will make you a more reliable leader — the kind people trust, follow, and depend on.

It's time to engineer clarity.
It's time to take responsibility for what others understand.
It's time to communicate with intention instead of assumption.

The pages that follow will show you how.

How to Use This 30-Day Guide

This book is not a script. It is not a collection of tips.
It is a **practice**—a way to retrain how you think about communication, how you prepare for it, and how you carry responsibility for the understanding others walk away with.

Each day offers one essential shift in how you shape meaning.
Because communication isn't the words you speak; it's the interpretation you create. And interpretation is never neutral—it is shaped by timing, context, emotion, workload, history, and the filters people don't even realize they're using.

The goal of this book is simple:
to help you engineer clarity on purpose.

You don't need to race through it.
Give each day space.
Start in the morning before urgency begins to compete for your attention.
Read slowly. Sit with it. Let the idea settle long enough to notice how it shows up in the way you send updates, assign work, respond to confusion, or clarify expectations.

By the time the day ends, look back at the conversations you had.
Where did clarity strengthen alignment?
Where did ambiguity invite drift?
Where did the responsibility for understanding fall—and did you carry it?

Communication – A 30-Day Mindsets Transformation Guide

Each day follows a consistent rhythm:

- **The Lesson** – A focused insight into a specific communication principle — the practical truth you must internalize to improve the reliability of your message.
- **The Reflection** – A prompt for awareness. Not to find fault, but to reveal patterns.
- **The Commitment** – A short statement to anchor your intention for the day. A signal to yourself of the leader you are choosing to be.
- **The EBR Principle** – A grounding truth: a reminder that communication is evidence-based work, and that every message, every update, and every moment of silence leaves a trail of results.

This rhythm matters more than speed.
These entries are intentionally brief—not to be skimmed, but to be absorbed before the day's noise demands your attention.

Some days will challenge the way you've always communicated.
Others will validate instincts you've had for years but never named.
The purpose is not to choose between empathy and precision, or between leadership and structure, but to merge them—to make communication both human and reliable.

Because communication doesn't live in templates or slides.
It lives in patterns—in the way you explain decisions, anticipate confusion, prevent drift, and verify alignment before it breaks.

Each time you read, reflect, and realign, you reduce uncertainty for the people who depend on you.

That is the daily work of clarity.
That is the discipline of evidence-based communication.
That is how you build a culture that communicates with intention—one mindset at a time.

Why the Emphasis on Mindsets?

Every improvement journey begins with a decision — and every decision begins with a mindset. Before you can change what people do, you have to change what they believe about what matters. That's why every book in this series starts with thinking, not tools. Procedures and policies don't stick if the people inside the system still see the world the same way.

Mindset is the hidden architecture of behavior — the lens through which we interpret data, make judgments, and justify choices. When the frame is wrong, the evidence doesn't matter. Leaders often install new methods on top of old mindsets, then wonder why the change collapses. Methods manage behavior. Mindsets determine it.

If you want different results, you must start upstream — with how people think about their work, their role, and their responsibility.

Mindset as the Bridge Between Human and System

Reliable organizations understand that mindset is the bridge between human leadership and system discipline. Systems give structure; mindsets give meaning. One without the other drifts.

Checks, audits, and communication loops only work when people believe the discipline itself matters. When people see safety or reliability as compliance, they work to avoid blame. When they see it as stewardship, they work to protect value. The process may look identical — but the mindset behind it changes everything.

Belief Before Behavior

Human performance research shows that people act their way into consistency, but believe their way into commitment. Beliefs shape what we notice, how we interpret risk, and what we feel responsible to do.

Change efforts built only on process often trigger resistance. When they begin with mindset, they invite reflection instead of defensiveness. Mindset work slows us down long enough to see our thinking — and once we can see it, we can choose it.

The Role of Reflection

Each day in this series uses reflection because reflection turns belief into evidence. It's easy to agree with a principle; it's harder to see where our own behavior quietly violates it.

The daily structure — The Moment, The Mindset, The Discipline, Reflection, Commitment — surfaces that gap. The goal is not guilt; it's growth. Real change comes from small, repeated recalibrations — a rhythm of awareness.

Evidence-Based Thinking

Mindset work is also evidence work. It replaces assumption with observation and story with pattern. When you treat your own reactions as data, you become both scientist and subject.

Evidence-based leaders look for behavioral patterns and adjust beliefs to match reality. These pages don't give rules; they offer mirrors — invitations to see clarity, consistency, or drift in your own environment.

The Outcome

When mindsets change, everything aligns faster. Communication sharpens. Systems gain purpose. Results finally match intent.

Mindset isn't the warm-up to the work — it *is* the work. It's how you close the gap between what you say and what you show. When leaders change how they think, they don't just create new systems — they create new possibilities.

THE EBR COMMUNICATION FRAMEWORK

Communication as the transfer of understanding, the management of meaning, and the reduction of uncertainty.

1. The Sender Owns the Burden of Communication

The central premise of EBR communication is simple and absolute:

The sender carries the full responsibility for ensuring understanding.
The receiver only acts on the understanding once it is made clear.

This means the sender must:

- Provide the right **context**
- Anchor that context in **evidence**
- Translate meaning into the **receiver's world**
- Anticipate filters that distort interpretation
- **Verify** how the message is understood
- Adjust until **alignment** is achieved
- Communicate **earlier than needed**
- Re-engage when **drift** appears

The receiver cannot detect their own misunderstanding.
They cannot ask for clarity on details they don't know exist.
They cannot translate meaning they have never been taught.

EBR communication begins with the leader accepting this fundamental responsibility.

2. Communication Must Be Anchored in Evidence, Not Assumption

Interpretation is what the receiver builds.
Evidence is what the sender provides.

- Evidence reduces noise
- Evidence stabilizes meaning
- Evidence prevents fear-based interpretation
- Evidence ensures the message begins with *what is true*

In EBR, **context is incomplete unless grounded in evidence.**

3. Alignment Requires Designing for Interpretation, Not Assuming It

People interpret messages through filters — emotions, workload, incentives, past experiences, and perceived risk.

The sender must design the message specifically for those filters.

3A. Speak in the Receiver's Terms

Meaning must be shaped using the receiver's vocabulary, mental model, and operational reality.

3B. The Meaning-Facilitator Role

In EBR, communicators are not crafters of messages — they are **engineers of meaning**.
They extract what matters, structure it clearly, and ensure it lands as intended.

4. Timing Must Be Earlier Than Needed

Understanding requires cognitive runway.
"Just-in-time communication" is miscommunication in disguise — it assumes instant interpretation and instant alignment.

Leaders communicate early because:

- Early gives time to think
- Early gives time to question
- Early gives time to align
- Early prevents drift and rework

Timing is part of the sender's responsibility.

5. Communication Effort Must Be Proportional to a Person's Role in the Outcome

Not everyone needs everything, and not everyone needs it at the same depth.

EBR Proportionality Principle:

Those with greater influence on the success of the work receive earlier, deeper, and more frequent communication.
Those with less influence receive a lighter, higher-level cadence.

Communication is engineered for relevance, not broadcast evenly.

6. The EBR Communication Structure

Every clear communication event follows a predictable sequence:

Context (with Evidence) → Interpretation → Implication → Required Action

- **Context (with Evidence)**
  What is happening and why it matters — grounded in signal, not story.
- **Interpretation**
  Meaning shaped intentionally in the receiver's terms.
- **Implication**
  What happens downstream if nothing changes — the reliability effect chain.
- **Required Action**
  What must happen next, by whom, and by when.
  This structure transforms communication into a repeatable discipline.

7. The EBR Alignment Loop

Understanding is not created once — it must be confirmed, aligned, and maintained.

Context (with Evidence) → Interpretation → Confirmation → Coordination → Drift Check

- **Confirmation**
  The sender validates the receiver's interpretation — not their agreement.
- **Coordination**
  Shared meaning becomes synchronized behavior.
- **Drift Check**
  Understanding decays over time.
  The sender must inspect, correct, and realign before misalignment becomes failure.

8. Communication Must Prevent Isolation and Produce Ownership

Solutions created in isolation generate resistance.
Solutions created *with* people generate ownership.

EBR communication:

- Prevents unilateral decision-making
- Creates opportunities for contribution and co-development
- Clarifies rationale, evidence, and impact
- Builds ownership through participation
- Ensures people understand what they are building and why

People support what they help build — communication is the mechanism that creates that support.

9. Communication Requires a Cadence of Accountability

EBR communication has rhythm:

- Regular check-ins
- Barrier removal
- Consequence reviews
- Reinforcement
- Drift detection
- Alignment resets

Cadence keeps the message stable as conditions change.

10. Communication Must Surface and Manage Unintended Consequences

Communication is an early-warning function.
It reveals:

- Downstream risks
- Resource conflicts
- Systemic effects
- Operational constraints
- Behavioral impacts

This prevents small misalignments from becoming systemic failures.

11. Alignment Is a Designed Outcome

Understanding is a product.
Clarity is engineered.
Alignment is intentional.

In the EBR worldview:

Communication is a reliability process.
Understanding is its product.
Alignment is its quality standard.

DAY 1 — The Sender Owns the Burden of Communication

The Lesson

Most breakdowns in work, performance, relationships, and culture come from one simple misunderstanding: people assume communication is a shared responsibility.
"It takes two."
"They should have asked."
"They should have spoken up."
"They should have known better."

But in the real world—especially in operational environments—people rarely know what they don't know.
They don't know what context is missing.
They don't know which details matter.
They don't know what assumptions they're making.
They don't know what questions to ask.

That's why communication begins with a non-negotiable truth:

The sender carries the burden for ensuring understanding.

Not half of it.
Not most of it.
All of it.

This isn't about control—it's about clarity.
The sender is the one connected to the full picture: the deeper context, the constraints, the consequences, the details, the timing, the downstream effects, the history, the "why," and the "what comes next."

The receiver sees only a small slice of that picture.
So expecting them to fill in the gaps is not fair—and it's not reliable.

Communication – A 30-Day Mindsets Transformation Guide

When communication fails, it almost always fails at the point where a leader *assumed* understanding instead of *engineering* it.
Great communicators don't wait for confusion to surface.
They design their message so that misunderstanding becomes unlikely.
They speak in the receiver's terms, verify interpretation, and check for drift over time.

Communication becomes a leadership discipline the moment you accept that clarity is your responsibility—not theirs.

The Reflection

Where have I expected others to understand something I didn't fully explain or clarify?
How many of my past frustrations were caused by the gap between what I meant and what others interpreted?
What changes when I begin treating understanding as something I am responsible for creating?

The Commitment

Today, I will take full responsibility for the clarity of my communication—before, during, and after the conversation occurs.
I will not assume understanding simply because I said the words.
I will ensure the message lands the way I intend.

EBR Principle

The sender carries the full burden for creating, verifying, and maintaining understanding.

DAY 2 — Communication Is the Transfer of Meaning, Not the Delivery of Words

The Lesson

Most people think communication happens at the moment they speak. They believe the act of saying the words — giving the instruction, sending the email, holding the meeting — is what creates clarity. But communication has never been about language alone. It has always been about meaning. And meaning lives not in the mouth of the speaker but in the mind of the listener.

The challenge is that meaning is fragile. It is shaped by filters the sender rarely sees: workload, fatigue, stress, assumptions, incentives, fears, personality, past experience, organizational history, and the listener's interpretation of what is truly being asked of them. A single message can travel through two different minds and emerge as two entirely different understandings — both sincerely believed, both confidently held, both potentially wrong.

This is why great communicators don't merely craft sentences; they craft context. They think in advance about how their words will land, not just how they will sound. They consider what the listener already knows, what they don't know, what they may be worried about, and what meaning they are likely to project into the gaps. They do the pre-work of shaping the environment, so the intended meaning becomes the most natural meaning.

And they verify. They reject the illusion that agreement equals understanding. They know a nod is not comprehension and silence is not alignment. They treat "How are you interpreting this?" as a normal part of leadership, not an optional courtesy.

When you shift from delivering information to transferring meaning, communication becomes a discipline of stewardship. You stop measuring success by what you said and start measuring success by what they understood. That's when communication turns into leadership.

Communication – A 30-Day Mindsets Transformation Guide

The Reflection

Think about a moment when you walked away from a conversation feeling confident you were clear, only to discover later that someone took action based on an entirely different understanding. What shaped their interpretation? Did they have different pressures, assumptions, or concerns than you realized? Were they missing context that seemed obvious to you but invisible to them?

Now imagine if, before that conversation, you had paused to consider how the message would sound from *their* vantage point. What questions might you have clarified up front? What assumptions might you have surfaced? How might the outcome have changed if your goal had been not to speak clearly, but to ensure the meaning landed exactly as intended?

The Commitment

- I will focus not on delivering information but on ensuring understanding.
- I will consider the listener's context before I speak, and I will verify meaning—not assume it.
- I will treat communication as a transfer of meaning, not a transmission of language.

EBR Principle

Communication succeeds only when the meaning in the sender's mind becomes the meaning in the receiver's mind.

DAY 3 — Assumptions Are the Silent Killers of Communication

The Lesson

Most communication failures don't come from bad intentions, poor skill, or lack of effort. They come from assumptions — the quiet, invisible shortcuts our brains take when we believe we already understand the situation, the other person, or the meaning behind the message. Assumptions are efficient, tempting, and almost always wrong in the places where accuracy matters most. They allow us to fill in missing details with our own experience, our own pressure, and our own point of view, long before we stop to verify whether any of it matches reality.

In operational environments, assumptions cause leaders to believe the team "knows the drill," "understands the priority," or "gets the why" without ever confirming it. They cause employees to interpret instructions based on habit instead of accuracy. They cause teams to carry out work under the illusion of alignment while quietly drifting toward consequences no one intended. And the worst part: assumptions feel like clarity. They feel like understanding. They feel like efficiency. That's what makes them dangerous.

Great communicators treat assumptions as hazards. They slow down at the exact moments others speed up. They ask clarifying questions even when they think they already know the answer. They build context instead of filling in blanks. They verify meaning instead of assuming it. They refuse to treat familiarity as understanding or repetition as alignment. And they recognize that assumptions do not show up as dramatic mistakes — they show up as small deviations that accumulate into major failures.

When you learn to see assumptions as threats, communication becomes more deliberate, more disciplined, and far more effective. You stop trusting what you think they know and start confirming what you both actually share. You replace guesswork with clarity — and clarity is the beginning of reliability.

The Reflection

Where have assumptions quietly shaped my communication this week? Did I assume someone understood a timeline, priority, or expectation simply because they've handled something similar before? Did I assume alignment because no one asked questions? Did I interpret someone's silence as agreement instead of uncertainty?

Think about how often you fill in gaps with your own logic, experience, or urgency. Now consider how the conversation might have changed if you had paused long enough to check the shared understanding. What friction, rework, or frustration could have been prevented by replacing even one assumption with one clarifying question?

The Commitment

- I will treat assumptions as risks.
- I will slow down at the moments when my brain wants to speed up.
- I will check for shared understanding instead of guessing at it.
- I will not assume clarity — I will confirm it.

EBR Principle

Assumptions destroy alignment. Verification creates it.

DAY 4 — Speak in the Receiver's Terms

The Lesson

One of the most overlooked truths in communication is this: people do not interpret messages based on the sender's world — they interpret them through their own. They hear your words, but they filter them through their priorities, pressures, vocabulary, context, incentives, fears, and lived experiences. When leaders communicate in their *own* terms — using their assumptions, their mental models, their shortcuts — misunderstandings become inevitable. But when leaders speak in the receiver's terms, meaning becomes accessible, accurate, and durable.

Speaking in the receiver's terms is not about simplifying. It is about translating. It is the discipline of entering someone else's world long enough to understand how they think, what they care about, what they fear getting wrong, and what language feels natural to them. It requires you to abandon the idea that "clear to me" equals "clear to them." It asks you to build meaning using the materials of *their* environment.

When you adapt your language to fit the receiver, several things happen. Confusion drops. Engagement rises. Responsibility becomes clearer. Priorities snap into focus. And alignment becomes a function of empathy rather than effort. People stop guessing what you meant and start taking action based on what they actually understand. This shift is not superficial — it is structural. It changes communication from a monologue into a connection.

The best communicators do this instinctively: they adjust vocabulary for frontline teams, translate strategy into daily behaviors, reframe complexity into relevance, and connect expectations to the world the listener actually lives in. They understand that communication is not about expressing your meaning — it is about ensuring *they* can use it.

The Reflection

Think of a time when you explained something that felt perfectly clear but landed flat, met confusion, or required rework. Were you speaking from *your* frame of reference or theirs? What vocabulary did you use that may have been familiar to you but foreign to them?

How might the message have changed if you had paused long enough to consider their workload, their priorities, their pressures, or the specific way their role interprets responsibility?

Consider how often misalignment is not caused by the message itself but by the gap between the world you spoke from and the world they heard from. What might shift if you made translation part of your leadership routine?

The Commitment

- I will speak in terms the receiver naturally uses and understands.
- I will shape my message around their role, their pressures, and their perspective — not my own.

EBR Principle

Clarity grows when leaders communicate from the listener's world, not their own.

DAY 5 — The Difference Between Information and Meaning

The Lesson

Most communication fails long before the words are spoken. It fails because leaders confuse *information* with *meaning* — assuming that once the facts have been shared, understanding will naturally follow. But information is only raw material. Meaning is the structure the listener builds from that material, using their own assumptions, experiences, pressures, and internal logic. And the moment information enters another person's mind, it begins to transform. It bends around their priorities. It mixes with what they think they already know. It fills the gaps with their fears, their interpretations, and their mental shortcuts. The sender delivers data; the receiver constructs a story.

This distinction matters because leaders often believe their job is to distribute information efficiently. They send emails quickly. They relay instructions clearly. They provide updates thoroughly. Yet none of that guarantees shared understanding. Information delivered is not the same as meaning received. A message explained is not the same as a message absorbed. Communication succeeds only when both people end up with the *same* meaning — and that requires more than transmission.

Great communicators recognize that meaning must be *built*, not assumed. They slow down long enough to shape interpretation. They answer the implicit questions: Why does this matter? What changes because of it? What should I do? What risk do we avoid? What expectation is shifting? They connect information to relevance, relevance to action, and action to outcomes. They understand that information without meaning creates confusion, but meaning built on information creates alignment.

When you treat meaning as something you are responsible for constructing — not something you hope emerges on its own — communication becomes intentional, not accidental.

The Reflection

Think about a time you shared information that seemed straightforward, only to discover that someone used it incorrectly, minimized its importance, or acted in a way you didn't expect.

What meaning did *they* build from the information you provided? What cues, context, or connections were missing? Consider how often you distribute information assuming others will interpret it as you do — even though their pressures, incentives, and mental models differ from yours.

What would shift if you treated information as the starting point of communication rather than the conclusion? How much rework, frustration, or drift could be avoided if you invested more energy in shaping the meaning that information is supposed to lead to?

The Commitment

- I will treat information as raw material and take responsibility for turning it into shared meaning.
- I will make the connection between what is said and what it *should* mean unmistakably clear.

EBR Principle

Information moves quickly; meaning must be built deliberately.

DAY 6 — Evidence as the Stabilizer of Meaning

The Lesson

Every conversation contains two forces: what is **observable** and what is **assumed**. The observable anchors the message; the assumed distorts it. When communication relies too heavily on interpretation, memory, emotion, or urgency, meaning becomes unstable — it shifts as it moves from person to person, meeting to meeting, and moment to moment. Evidence is what prevents that drift. It is the stabilizer. It converts a message from something subjective and variable into something concrete, repeatable, and verifiable.

Without evidence, people fill in the gaps with whatever feels most familiar: their past experiences, their fears, their frustrations, their workload, or their best guesses about what the leader "must be getting at." This guesswork is not malicious — it is human. Our brains crave closure, so in the absence of signal, they create their own. That's why vague messages spread differently across a team: one person hears danger, another hears urgency, another hears criticism, and another hears nothing at all. The original message dissolves, replaced by story.

Great communicators use evidence to prevent this collapse. They bring the conversation back to what is *real*: a number, a condition, a measurement, a timestamp, a deviation, a trend, an observable fact. Evidence makes the message sturdy. It reduces emotional noise. It limits projection. And it gives every person in the conversation the same starting point — not the illusion of a shared starting point, but an actual one grounded in reality.

Evidence doesn't replace judgment, but it guides it. It doesn't silence interpretation, but it shapes it. It turns communication into a disciplined process rather than a free-floating exchange of impressions. When leaders anchor meaning in evidence, misunderstandings shrink, alignment strengthens, and communication becomes resilient instead of fragile.

The Reflection

Think about a conversation where meaning slipped — where someone interpreted your words more strongly, more negatively, or more casually than you intended.

What evidence could have grounded that message and stabilized the interpretation? Consider the times you've communicated based on feeling, urgency, or general impression. How much did the lack of concrete signal open the door for misalignment?

Go reflect on your own tendency to rely on "everyone knows," "we've been seeing," or "it feels like" — and how different the outcome might have been if you had paused to anchor the conversation in something observable, specific, and real. Evidence doesn't just strengthen your argument; it strengthens their understanding.

The Commitment

- I will ground my communication in observable evidence.
- Before sharing a message, I will identify the signal — the fact, metric, or condition that stabilizes meaning — and use it to anchor interpretation.

EBR Principle

Evidence anchors interpretation. Communication becomes durable when it begins with what is real.

DAY 7 — Context Is Never Complete Without Evidence

The Lesson

Context is essential to communication — it explains purpose, direction, and intent. But context alone is not enough. Without evidence, context becomes vulnerable to drift. It turns into story, speculation, or assumption masquerading as clarity. People begin filling the gaps with their own interpretations, memories, frustrations, or fears, and the message becomes a moving target rather than a stable anchor. Leaders often believe they are providing clarity when they explain the "why," the history, or the surrounding circumstances. But if the explanation is not grounded in something observable and real, the listener interprets it through their own lens and meaning fractures.

Evidence is what completes context. It is the stabilizing force that prevents narrative from overtaking truth. When you connect context to signal — a measurement, a trend, a deviation, a timestamp, an observed behavior, a specific condition — you give the listener something solid to stand on. You narrow the range of possible interpretations. You make the message harder to distort and easier to align around. Without evidence, context becomes a story about what might be happening. With evidence, context becomes a statement about what *is* happening.

Leaders sometimes avoid evidence unintentionally. They rely on tone, urgency, or emphasis, believing the importance will be obvious. But urgency without evidence feels like pressure, and pressure without clarity breeds resistance. Other times, leaders assume the frontline "already knows the data," not realizing how disconnected different levels of the organization can be. Evidence equalizes the conversation. It gives everyone the same frame, the same starting point, and the same definition of reality.

When context and evidence travel together, communication becomes both human and precise. The listener knows not just *why* something matters, but *what* proves it matters. And that changes everything.

The Reflection

Think about recent conversations where you provided context — explaining the situation, the urgency, or the reasoning — but didn't anchor your message in evidence.

How did others interpret what you said? Did they overreact, underreact, or fill the gaps with assumptions?

Reflect on how often you expect people to connect the dots from context alone, without showing them the observable signal that gives the context weight. What would have shifted if you had brought data, a real example, a measurement, or a specific incident into the conversation? How much rework, disagreement, or confusion might have been avoided if the context had been paired with proof?

The Commitment

- I will not provide context without pairing it with evidence that stabilizes the message.
- I will anchor my explanations in something observable so interpretation cannot drift.
- I will ensure people know not just *why* something matters, but *what* proves it matters.
- I will use evidence to align understanding before urgency enters the conversation.

EBR Principle

Context explains why; evidence proves why. Together, they create meaning that does not drift.

DAY 8 — Reducing Noise by Using Observables

The Lesson

Noise is the enemy of clarity. It shows up in the form of assumptions, opinions, emotions, incomplete memories, competing priorities, vague warnings, and the stories people tell themselves when the truth is not yet clear. The more noise present in a conversation, the more likely the message will drift from person to person, hour to hour, or meeting to meeting. Noise causes people to overreact, underreact, misinterpret, catastrophize, minimize, or assign meaning based on whatever is most familiar rather than what is actually true.

Observables are how leaders reduce that noise. Observables are the facts that can be seen, measured, pointed to, or verified without interpretation: a number on a dashboard, a temperature reading, a missed handoff, a condition on a piece of equipment, a timestamp, a deviation from standard, a pattern in the data, or a documented behavior. Observables quiet the emotional static that often accompanies communication. They shrink the space where fear and imagination thrive. They tell people, "Here is what is real. Here is what we know. Here is what we can act on."

Noise increases anxiety. Observables reduce it. Noise invites guesswork. Observables replace it with grounding. Noise fractures alignment. Observables unify interpretation because they give everyone the same anchor point. When leaders communicate without observables, people create their own mental models — and those models often conflict. But when observables lead the message, interpretation becomes more stable, predictable, and accurate.

Great communicators use observables as a discipline. They begin with what is visible before discussing what is possible. They separate what is known from what is assumed. They use facts to guide emotion, not the other way around. And they understand that observables do not make communication cold — they make it trustworthy.

The Reflection

Think about a recent moment when noise overtook clarity — a situation where people got nervous, confused, reactive, or defensive because the signal wasn't clear.

What observables could have anchored the conversation early? Reflect on times when a team filled in the gaps with speculation because no one had put the facts on the table yet. How much energy was wasted managing fear, assumptions, or backchannel interpretation that never needed to exist in the first place?

Consider your own tendencies: do you sometimes communicate urgency or concern before grounding the message in what is objectively observable? How might outcomes change if you filtered noise through observables before speaking?

The Commitment

- I will begin my communication with what is observable before discussing what it means.
- I will use concrete facts to reduce emotional noise and stabilize interpretation.
- I will separate what is known from what is assumed, and I will help others do the same.
- I will anchor conversations in reality so that clarity becomes the default, not the exception.

EBR Principle

Observables quiet noise. When facts lead, fear and guesswork lose their power.

DAY 9 — Signal vs. Story

The Lesson

Human beings are natural storytellers. The moment we encounter a piece of information — a metric, a comment, an observation, a delay, a deviation — our brains rush to explain it. The explanation feels instantaneous, automatic, and accurate. But it is almost always a story, not a signal. A signal is what happened. A story is what we think it means. And unless leaders learn to separate the two, communication becomes clouded by interpretation disguised as truth.

Signals are objective: a temperature increased, a deadline slipped, a step was skipped, a downtime event occurred, a customer called, a trend changed. Stories are subjective: "They weren't paying attention," "They don't care," "Maintenance is falling behind," "Operations is rushing," "Leadership isn't listening." Stories feel satisfying because they provide closure. But closure is not clarity. Clarity requires discipline — the discipline to pause before assigning meaning, to interrogate the signal before constructing a narrative, and to acknowledge that our first interpretation is often the product of pressure, frustration, or habit rather than evidence.

Great communicators build the habit of holding the signal still. They resist the urge to explain too quickly. They ask: *What do I actually know? What am I assuming? What story am I adding? What interpretation am I projecting onto this?* This slows the drift between what is real and what is imagined. It also prevents leaders from communicating emotion as if it were fact — a common and destructive mistake.

When leaders confuse story for signal, they communicate judgment rather than clarity. They create defensiveness rather than alignment. They speak from assumption rather than truth. But when leaders separate signal from story, communication becomes grounded, accurate, and actionable. People know what actually happened, not what someone guessed happened. And meaning becomes something constructed together rather than imposed by the loudest interpretation in the room.

The Reflection

Think of a moment recently when you reacted quickly — to a message, a number, a behavior, or a delay. What story did you attach to the signal? How quickly did your mind move from "what happened" to "why it happened," "who caused it," or "what it reveals"? Reflect on how rarely we pause to examine the difference between the two.

What conversations this week would have changed if you had slowed down and named the signal before exploring the story? What conflict, frustration, or misalignment might have been avoided if others had heard the observable fact instead of your interpretation of it?

Consider how many communication failures are not failures of information but failures of meaning-making that began too early and too confidently.

The Commitment

- I will name the signal before I name the story.
- I will separate what I know from what I am assuming.
- I will hold interpretation loosely until evidence supports it.
- I will communicate reality, not projection.

EBR Principle

Signals tell you what happened. Stories tell you what you fear, assume, or expect. Leaders must know the difference.

DAY 10 — Evidence Before Urgency

The Lesson

Urgency is powerful — and dangerous — when used incorrectly. When a leader communicates urgency without evidence, the message becomes pressure without clarity. People feel pushed but don't understand why. They respond with stress instead of precision. They act quickly instead of acting correctly. And urgency, meant to accelerate alignment, ends up accelerating confusion.

Urgency is only productive when it is grounded in something real. Evidence is what gives urgency legitimacy. It shows the team *why* speed matters, *what* risk is emerging, *where* deviation is occurring, and *how* the situation is changing. When urgency arrives without proof, people fill in the blanks with fear, assumptions, or worst-case stories. They brace for impact rather than preparing for action. And over time, urgency becomes background noise — something leaders say when they want movement rather than when movement is truly required.

Great communicators understand that urgency is a tool, not a habit. They do not use it casually. They do not confuse their own stress with organizational necessity. They show the evidence first: the trend that is shifting, the KPI that is dropping, the condition that is worsening, the backlog that is rising, the constraint that is tightening. Only then do they communicate the urgency — and by that point, the team already feels it. Evidence creates shared reality. Shared reality creates shared urgency. And shared urgency produces coordinated action instead of frantic motion.

When you communicate evidence before urgency, people move for the right reasons, not the loudest ones. They act with purpose instead of pressure. They make decisions aligned with the signal instead of the emotion. And urgency becomes not a shout, but a cue — a cue to respond with discipline.

Communication – A 30-Day Mindsets Transformation Guide

The Reflection

Think about the last time you communicated urgency: a missed deadline, a shift in production, an equipment concern, a customer escalation, a staffing challenge.

Did you show evidence first, or did you jump straight into emotion, frustration, or emphasis? How did the team react? Did they move with understanding or with stress? Reflect on how often urgency is used to motivate when clarity would have done the job better. How much misalignment has been caused by urgency delivered before proof?

Consider how different the response might have been if you had grounded the message in observable signal before communicating the pressure.

The Commitment

- I will communicate evidence before urgency.
- I will ensure people see the signal that justifies the call to action.
- I will not use pressure as a substitute for clarity.
- I will reserve urgency for situations where the evidence demands it.

EBR Principle

Urgency without evidence creates pressure; urgency with evidence creates alignment.

DAY 11 — Interpretation Is the Failure Point

The Lesson

Most leaders believe communication fails at the moment the words are spoken — the wrong phrasing, the unclear sentence, the missing detail. But the real failure point comes later, often silently, when the listener begins to interpret what was said. Interpretation is where communication succeeds or collapses. It is the moment the message stops belonging to the sender and starts becoming something new inside the mind of the receiver.

Interpretation is not a neutral process. It is filtered through past experiences, fears, frustrations, incentives, priorities, stress, culture, and the stories people tell themselves about how the organization works. Two people can hear the same message and reconstruct completely different meanings — both with total confidence. This is not a sign of incompetence; it is a sign of being human. Interpretation is inevitable. The question is never whether interpretation will happen. The question is whether the sender guides it or allows it to drift.

When leaders ignore interpretation, communication becomes a gamble: *Will they understand what I meant? Will they take the right action? Will this message hold under pressure?* When leaders take ownership of interpretation, communication becomes a process: *How will this land? What meaning will they build? What assumptions will they bring? How do I guide them toward the meaning that matches reality and intention?*

Great communicators assume that meaning will distort unless they intentionally shape it. They design messages that anticipate misinterpretation. They clarify the core point before details. They check understanding before alignment. They ask questions that expose how the message has been reconstructed. And they treat interpretation not as the listener's responsibility, but as the sender's domain.

Interpretation is the failure point because it is the moment the message transforms. Leaders who don't manage that transformation lose clarity. Leaders who do manage it build reliability.

The Reflection

Think back to a moment when someone acted on your message, and the action was technically reasonable but fundamentally misaligned with what you intended.

What interpretation did they build? What assumptions did they use to fill the gaps? How quickly did their brain move from "what was said" to "what this must mean for me"?

Now consider how often you trust your delivery instead of verifying their interpretation. How much drift, rework, conflict, or inefficiency has come not from what you communicated but from how it was interpreted? What would change if you treated interpretation as the stage where your leadership matters most?

The Commitment

- I will design my communication with interpretation in mind — not just information.
- I will anticipate how meaning might drift and address those gaps before they form.
- I will verify understanding rather than assuming it.
- I will take responsibility for guiding interpretation, not leaving it to chance.

EBR Principle

Interpretation is where communication fails — unless the sender takes responsibility for shaping it.

DAY 12 — Meaning-Making as a Leadership Skill

The Lesson

Most leaders think communication ends once the message is spoken. But communication doesn't end at delivery — it ends at meaning. Meaning-making is the unseen work that determines whether a message becomes clarity, confusion, urgency, or indifference. And meaning is never automatic. It must be shaped. In every organization, the people who interpret the message end up controlling the outcome. That is why meaning-making is not a soft skill — it is a leadership skill, and one of the most decisive.

Every listener constructs meaning using the mental tools they already possess: their past wins and failures, their fears, their workload, their belief about how decisions are made, and the unwritten rules of the culture. Even the most precise message becomes vulnerable once it enters that environment. Without guidance, meaning drifts toward convenience, habit, or self-protection — not toward alignment. Leaders who treat interpretation as "their responsibility, not mine" accidentally delegate meaning-making to the very forces they spend their careers trying to control.

Great communicators take the opposite approach. They see meaning-making as part of their job — a responsibility as real as setting direction or allocating resources. They slow down long enough to shape how the message should be understood before they push for action. They define what the message *is*, what it *is not*, and what it *changes*. They anchor the meaning before they introduce the details, knowing that people cannot follow what they do not correctly interpret.

Meaning-making is leadership because meaning determines movement. When leaders guide interpretation intentionally, teams respond with confidence instead of hesitation, coordination instead of fragmentation. When leaders abdicate meaning-making, the organization is forced to guess — and guessing is rarely aligned, consistent, or repeatable. Meaning does not form by accident. Leaders must build it.

The Reflection

Think about a time when your message was technically clear, yet the outcome still missed the mark. What meaning did the listener construct? What fears, assumptions, or past patterns shaped their interpretation? What part of the message needed your guidance — not in the words themselves, but in how they should have been *understood*?

Now consider your daily communication. How often do you communicate information but leave the meaning unstated? How much alignment, speed, or confidence would you gain if you treated meaning-making as a required step — not an optional one?

The Commitment

- I will define the meaning of my message before expecting action.
- I will guide how the message should be understood — not leave meaning to chance.
- I will make explicit what the message *is* and what it *is not*.
- I will take responsibility for shaping meaning as a core leadership discipline.

EBR Principle

Meaning does not emerge on its own — the sender must build it before the listener can act on it.

DAY 13 — Designing Messages for Human Filters

The Lesson

Every person receives a message through a set of filters that you cannot see but must account for: workload, stress, incentives, fear, confidence, past experiences, and cultural norms. These filters don't simply color the message — they reshape it. They determine what stands out, what gets ignored, what feels urgent, what feels risky, and what meaning is constructed before action is taken. If leaders don't design communication with these filters in mind, they unintentionally design it for failure.

Human filters operate automatically and instantly. A stressed employee hears urgency even when none is stated. A burned-out team hears blame even when the message is neutral. A high-performer hears opportunity. A fearful employee hears threat. Communication is never delivered into a vacuum; it is delivered into lived experience. This is why leaders who communicate only from their own perspective unintentionally speak to an audience that doesn't exist.

Designing messages for human filters doesn't require manipulation — it requires empathy and precision. Great communicators slow down to consider the conditions shaping the listener's mindset. They anticipate how incentives might distort meaning, how fear might shrink interpretation, and how past failures might overshadow the present message. Then they shape their communication to land inside the reality the listener occupies, not the one the leader imagines.

When leaders design with filters in mind, communication becomes more stable, more predictable, and more aligned. When they ignore those filters, clarity becomes fragile. Designing for human filters is not about being careful — it is about being effective.

The Reflection

Think of someone on your team whose interpretation of messages consistently differs from your intent. What filters are shaping their world — pressure, fear, habit, or exhaustion? How much of their misunderstanding comes from the message itself, and how much comes from the environment they're interpreting it through?

Now consider your last important communication. Did you design it for your perspective or theirs? How would the message shift if it were crafted for the listener's actual filters rather than your mental model of them?

The Commitment

- I will design messages for the listener's reality, not my own.
- I will anticipate the filters that could distort meaning.
- I will communicate in ways that respect workload, incentives, and stress.
- I will shape messages to reduce distortion before it appears.

EBR Principle

Communication succeeds when it is designed for the filters that shape meaning.

DAY 14 — The Receiver Cannot Detect Their Own Misunderstanding

The Lesson

One of the most overlooked realities in communication is this: the receiver cannot detect their own misunderstanding. Once a person reconstructs the message in their mind, that version becomes their truth. They don't see it as an interpretation — they see it as *the* meaning. And because it feels coherent, reasonable, and complete, they have no internal signal that anything is missing or incorrect. This makes misunderstanding uniquely dangerous: it hides inside certainty.

The brain is wired to favor closure over accuracy. The moment an interpretation "makes sense," the cognitive search stops. Details fade. Doubt quiets. The person moves forward confidently, unaware that their interpretation is misaligned. From their perspective, they are doing exactly what was asked. From the leader's perspective, the outcome looks careless, inattentive, or defiant. But it isn't — it's simply invisible misinterpretation running the show.

This dynamic is why so much misalignment feels sudden. It rarely comes from a dramatic failure. It comes from small misunderstandings that went unchallenged because both parties believed understanding existed. The sender assumed clarity because nothing sounded confused. The receiver assumed correctness because nothing felt confusing. And in that shared silence, drift quietly grows.

Great communicators refuse to rely on the listener's ability to self-diagnose misunderstanding. They understand that confidence is not proof of comprehension. They see verification not as a courtesy but as a core leadership responsibility. They check interpretation early, often, and without apology. They make it normal to clarify, normal to summarize, normal to restate, and normal to correct course before misunderstanding becomes momentum in the wrong direction. Misunderstanding cannot reveal itself — so the sender must surface actively seek it.

The Reflection

Think of a time when someone acted incorrectly yet sincerely believed they were doing exactly what you intended. What internal logic made their interpretation feel right to them? How long did they operate from that misplaced confidence before the gap became visible? And how much frustration or rework grew from a misunderstanding that neither of you could see in the moment?

Now consider how often you assume understanding simply because someone nods, agrees, or appears comfortable. How much alignment would you gain if you treated misunderstanding as silent and self-concealing? What would change in your communication if you assumed the listener cannot detect their own misinterpretation — and built validation into your process accordingly?

The Commitment

- I will never confuse confidence with comprehension.
- I will verify interpretation instead of waiting for misunderstanding to reveal itself.
- I will normalize clarification, so people feel safe uncovering what they don't yet see.
- I will treat verification as essential to alignment, not optional or polite.

EBR Principle

Misunderstanding hides inside certainty — which is why the sender must surface it.

DAY 15 — "Tell Me How You're Interpreting This"

The Lesson

The most reliable way to prevent communication failure is deceptively simple: ask the listener to show you how they understood the message. **"Tell me how you're interpreting this."** With that one question, leaders unlock the only perspective that truly matters — the meaning created in the listener's mind. This question is not about repeating your words back; it is about revealing the logic, assumptions, fears, and conclusions the listener built from those words. It exposes the difference between what was said and what was received.

Most leaders skip this step because the conversation *feels* clear. The listener nods. They agree. They repeat a keyword or two. It all appears aligned. But surface agreement is an unreliable indicator of true interpretation. People often signal understanding because they want to appear competent, avoid dragging out the meeting, or maintain forward momentum. None of those signals tell you whether they built the right meaning. Interpretation lives deeper than affirmation — and this question is the tool that reveals it.

Asking someone how they are interpreting the message requires humility from the leader. It is the willingness to discover that your explanation was incomplete. It is the discipline to adjust instead of defend. And it is the courage to slow down before speed generates rework. Leaders who use this question consistently view communication as a process, not a performance. They are not trying to impress the listener with clarity — they are trying to confirm alignment with reality.

Over time, this question reshapes team culture. People stop pretending they understand. They become more comfortable surfacing gaps early. Misalignment shrinks, not because misunderstandings no longer occur, but because they are caught before they become costly. When "Tell me how you're interpreting this" becomes normal, communication becomes safer, more honest, and more reliable. It is the quality control step that closes the distance between intention and interpretation — every time.

The Reflection

Think of a moment when you believed your message was clear, only to discover later that the listener built a very different meaning. If you had paused and asked, "Tell me how you're interpreting this," what mismatch would have surfaced? How much tension, rework, or lost time might have been prevented simply by checking the meaning before action?

Now reflect on your own communication habits. How often do you rely on agreement instead of interpretation? What patterns on your team show that people may be acting confidently on incomplete understanding? What would shift if you made this question a standard part of every important conversation?

The Commitment

- I will use "Tell me how you're interpreting this" as a routine leadership tool.
- I will inspect meaning rather than infer alignment.
- I will create a culture where clarification is expected, not embarrassing.
- I will treat verification as a structural part of communication, not an extra.

EBR Principle

Interpretation must be inspected — not assumed.

DAY 16 — The EBR Communication Structure

The Lesson

Most communication breaks because it is delivered as a stream of thoughts rather than as a disciplined sequence. The EBR Communication Structure — **Context (with Evidence) → Interpretation → Implication → Required Action** — exists to prevent that breakdown. It gives the sender a repeatable pattern for shaping meaning, guiding understanding, and ensuring that every message ends in aligned behavior. When leaders follow this structure, communication stops being a guess and becomes a system.

It starts with **Context and Evidence**, the stabilizers of meaning. People cannot interpret accurately unless they understand what is real, observable, and already known. Without evidence, the brain fills in gaps using emotion, fear, or past stories. With evidence, the message becomes anchored. Context tells people where they are; evidence tells them what is true. It's the starting point for reliable interpretation.

Next is **Interpretation**, the step most leaders assume will take care of itself. Interpretation is where meaning forms — and meaning determines movement. When leaders guide interpretation explicitly, they prevent drift before it begins. They clarify what the message *is*, what it *is not*, and how it should be understood in the listener's world. This step is not optional; it is the core of communication design.

Then comes **Implication**, the bridge between understanding and action. Implications answer the downstream questions: What changes? Who is affected? What risk increases? What gets delayed? What becomes newly important? Leaders who ignore implications leave people aligned in the moment but misaligned in execution. Thinking downstream prevents surprise, friction, and escalation.

Finally, the structure lands on **Required Action** — the operational anchor. No message is complete until the next step is unmistakable. What do you need them to do? When? How? Based on what standard? Ending with action ensures that clarity becomes movement instead of memory. The structure works because it creates order, reduces ambiguity, and produces alignment that holds even under pressure.

The Reflection

Think back to a recent communication that produced confusion or misalignment. Which element of the structure did you skip — context, interpretation, implication, or required action? How did that single omission open the door to drift or incorrect assumptions? How much friction or rework would have been prevented if the message had followed this sequence?

Now consider the last week of your communication. How often did you give direction without evidence, meaning without framing, or action without clarifying implications? What would change in your leadership if you treated this structure not as a tool for special situations, but as a standard operating rhythm?

The Commitment

- I will use the EBR Communication Structure to shape meaning intentionally.
- I will begin with evidence, so people interpret from truth, not fear.
- I will clarify implications so downstream effects are understood.
- I will end every important message with a clear required action.

EBR Principle

Structure turns communication from hopeful into reliable.

DAY 17 — Why Every Message Must End with Action

The Lesson

Communication is not complete when the listener understands your words; it is complete when the listener knows exactly what to do next. Too many messages end with shared awareness instead of shared action — and awareness without direction becomes drift. People walk away understanding the situation but unclear about movement. They agree with the premise but not the plan. They feel informed but not aligned. Clarity without action is communication left unfinished.

Humans default to their own patterns unless given a deliberate path. When a message ends without an action anchor, the listener fills the gap with their personal judgment, habits, prior experiences, or assumptions about what you want. This is where misalignment is born — not in the content of the message, but in the absence of direction. Two people who understand the same facts may still take completely different actions simply because the message ended before the path was defined.

Great communicators recognize that action is the point of communication, not the afterthought. They know that every message — whether it's an update, a warning, a clarification, or a strategic shift — must answer a simple, grounding question: *"What must happen now?"* Even if the required action is to pause, wait, observe, escalate, or hold steady, naming it prevents improvisation. Action is the organizing force that transforms understanding into alignment.

Ending with action is not about control; it is about coherence. It ensures that people move together, not separately. It ensures that interpretation leads somewhere predictable, not somewhere convenient. It ensures that the message produces results rather than noise. Leaders who end their messages with action build organizations that move with direction, rhythm, and confidence — not guesswork.

The Reflection

Think of a time when you gave a message that seemed clear, yet people took different paths afterward. What action did you leave unstated? How did the absence of a clear next step invite assumptions, hesitation, or conflicting priorities? How much confusion or rework would have been avoided if you had simply ended the message with a definitive "Here's what needs to happen next"?

Now reflect on your daily communication. How often do you explain, discuss, or inform without explicitly naming the action you expect? What would shift in your team's consistency and speed if every important message ended with a clear, unambiguous next step?

The Commitment

- I will never end important communication without naming the next action.
- I will clarify expectations so understanding becomes movement, not drift.
- I will ensure that direction is explicit, not implied or assumed.
- I will treat action as the final step of clarity, not an optional add-on.

EBR Principle

Clarity becomes real only when it becomes action.

DAY 18 — Implications: Thinking Downstream

The Lesson

Most leaders communicate with the immediate moment in mind — what needs to be said, what needs to be clarified, what needs to be corrected. But communication does not live only in the present; it creates a chain of consequences that unfold downstream. **Implications** are the hidden currents that determine how a message moves through priorities, responsibilities, timelines, and relationships. When leaders fail to articulate implications, they leave people aligned at the surface but misaligned in execution.

Every message changes something: workload, timing, risk, ownership, expectations, or coordination. If those changes are not named, the listener fills in the blanks with their own logic. One person assumes the work must start immediately. Another believes it can wait. One thinks it affects only their task. Another believes it requires a shift in the whole team's plan. None of these interpretations are irrational — they are simply unspoken implications being improvised. And improvisation is where drift grows.

Great communicators understand that clarity is not complete until the downstream effects are visible. They think beyond the message itself and consider the chain reaction it creates. What does this update change about priority? What does this instruction change about schedule? What does this decision change about who must be involved? Thinking downstream is not about predicting everything — it is about preventing the predictable misunderstandings that occur when people lack the full picture.

When leaders routinely articulate implications, they reduce friction dramatically. People stop stepping on each other's work. Stress decreases because expectations are explicit. Coordination strengthens because everyone understands not just the message, but its impact on the system around them. Implications transform communication from isolated statements into integrated guidance — the kind that actually produces aligned behavior.

The Reflection

Think about a recent situation where someone acted correctly from their point of view but incorrectly from yours. What implication did they miss because it was never named? How far downstream did that misunderstanding travel before it surfaced as conflict or rework? And how would the outcome have changed if you had articulated how the message affected timelines, priorities, or responsibilities?

Now consider your communication habits. How often do you state the message but skip the downstream effects? How much stronger, calmer, and more coordinated would your team be if implications were part of every important conversation?

The Commitment

- I will name the downstream effects of my messages, not leave them to assumption.
- I will make implications visible so alignment extends beyond the moment.
- I will guide how priorities, timelines, and responsibilities shift because of the message.
- I will treat implications as part of clarity, not a separate conversation.

EBR Principle

Communication becomes alignment when the downstream effects are made explicit.

DAY 19 — Coordination Instead of Compliance

The Lesson

Most organizations unintentionally design communication for compliance: "Do this," "Change that," "Focus here." It creates movement, but not alignment. People complete tasks, but they don't connect with each other. They follow instructions, but they don't synchronize. Compliance produces obedience; **coordination produces results**. And the difference lies in how leaders communicate. Compliance asks individuals to act. Coordination ensures the *team* moves together.

When communication is built around compliance, each person listens only for what affects them directly. They walk away thinking, *"What do I need to do?"* That question is useful, but incomplete. It leaves the broader system invisible. It creates siloed action — people executing their part without understanding how their decisions intersect with others. Even well-intended effort becomes friction. Compliance gets tasks done, but often at the cost of rework, overlap, or missed dependencies.

Great communicators design messages that build a shared mental model, not isolated instructions. They make visible how one action affects another. They name who needs to coordinate, who needs to signal, and who needs to adjust. They encourage people to think beyond individual execution and toward collective impact. Coordination is not softer than compliance — it is more disciplined, more intelligent, and more operationally effective. It prevents the chaos that arises when everyone interprets direction alone.

When teams are coordinated, they don't just act — they anticipate. They understand how their work influences timing, risk, and flow for others. They adjust early instead of waiting for problems to collide. Communication stops being a transaction and becomes a network. Leaders who communicate for coordination create organizations that don't just go faster; they go in the *same direction* at the *same time* — which is where real performance lives.

The Reflection

Think about a time when your team completed exactly what you asked, yet the overall outcome still fell short. What coordination was missing? Who acted correctly on their own but unknowingly created friction for someone else? How might the message have changed if you had framed it not as "Here's what you do" but as "Here's how we move together"?

Now consider your recent communication. How often do you give direction that only addresses the individual? How frequently do you leave the relational, shared, or interconnected parts unstated? What would shift if every message helped people see the system, not just their slice of it?

The Commitment

- I will communicate in ways that align people with each other, not just with my instructions.
- I will define how work connects across roles so action becomes coordinated, not isolated.
- I will help people see the system their decisions affect.
- I will treat coordination as the true measure of aligned communication.

EBR Principle

Compliance moves individuals — coordination moves the organization.

DAY 20 — Preventing Isolation in Communication

The Lesson

Communication often fails not because the message is unclear, but because it is delivered into isolation. When people receive information alone — without visibility into who else knows, who else is acting, or how their decisions affect the larger effort — they begin to operate as independent units rather than interconnected contributors. Isolation creates fragmentation. Fragmentation creates drift. And drift, once it begins, accelerates quietly until leaders wonder why everyone seems to be working hard but moving in different directions.

Humans do not naturally assume coordination; they assume autonomy. When a message is delivered individually, the listener interprets it individually. They focus on their task, their schedule, their priorities, their risks. This is not selfishness — it is instinct. Without explicit communication about shared expectations, people default to acting within the boundaries they can see. The moment communication isolates, execution isolates with it.

Great communicators prevent isolation by widening the frame. They make it clear who else is involved, what others are doing, and how decisions intersect across roles and functions. They do not assume people will "connect the dots." They connect the dots for them. They communicate not just the message, but the ecosystem the message lives within. This creates shared understanding, reduces unintentional conflict, and eliminates the friction that comes from well-intended people unknowingly working at cross-purposes.

Preventing isolation is not about meetings or broadcasts — it is about shared visibility. People need to know: Who else is affected? Who must be aware? Who needs to coordinate? Who must adjust if conditions change? When communication actively prevents isolation, organizations move with less noise, less drama, and less cleanup. People stop acting alone because they stop *thinking* alone. Clarity becomes collective instead of individual.

The Reflection

Think of a time when someone made a reasonable decision that still disrupted the broader effort. How much of that misstep came from isolation — from them not knowing who else was involved, what others were planning, or how their actions would intersect downstream? How different would the outcome have been if the communication had included shared visibility instead of individual direction?

Now reflect on your recent leadership communication. How often do you speak to individuals without clarifying the network around them? How often do you assume people know who else is affected? What would change if every important message expanded the frame instead of narrowing it?

The Commitment

- I will communicate in ways that prevent people from acting in isolation.
- I will make visible who else is involved and how roles intersect.
- I will ensure people understand the broader system their decisions affect.
- I will widen the frame of communication so clarity becomes shared, not solitary.

EBR Principle

Communication fails in isolation — and succeeds in shared visibility.

DAY 21 — Drift: Communication's Silent Failure Mode

The Lesson

Most communication does not fail in the moment it is delivered. It fails slowly, quietly, and almost imperceptibly over time. This gradual decay of shared understanding is **drift** — the silent failure mode of communication. Drift occurs when people continue acting on yesterday's meaning while reality, conditions, priorities, or interpretations shift around them. No one notices at first. Nothing looks wrong. But inch by inch, alignment loosens until the team is no longer operating from the same version of truth.

Drift is inevitable in human systems because memories fade, assumptions creep in, and context evolves. The brain compresses information, simplifies details, and reconstructs meaning for speed, not accuracy. Even the most aligned message begins to degrade the moment people return to their routines. They fill small gaps with personal logic. They adjust a detail here or there to fit their workflow. They interpret changes through the lens of habit. None of this is malicious — it is cognitive efficiency at work. But efficiency without calibration produces divergence.

Organizations that ignore drift experience recurring confusion that feels mysterious: "We talked about this." "We agreed on this." "We clarified this." And they did — at the time. But communication is not a one-time event; it is a state that requires maintenance. Drift is what happens when leaders assume that understanding remains intact simply because it once existed. In reality, understanding decays unless intentionally checked.

Great communicators treat drift as predictable and preventable. They do not expect messages to hold indefinitely. They revisit expectations, re-anchor meaning, refresh context, and confirm alignment before small deviations accumulate into costly detours. They understand that preventing drift is not re-explaining — it is re-stabilizing. It is the routine work of ensuring that clarity stays current, that direction remains shared, and that interpretation stays aligned with reality rather than memory.

The Reflection

Think of a time when a team slowly veered off course even though the original message was clear. What small shifts, assumptions, or compressions began the drift? How long did the misalignment grow unnoticed before it produced confusion, conflict, or rework? And what simple check-ins or recalibrations might have kept the understanding intact?

Now consider your own communication. How often do you assume that because something was understood once, it is still understood now? How much smoother would your operations run if you treated drift as a natural force — one you must anticipate and counteract intentionally?

The Commitment

- I will assume drift occurs unless actively prevented.
- I will refresh shared meaning before small deviations grow into dysfunction.
- I will maintain alignment through recalibration, not repetition.
- I will treat drift management as essential to sustained clarity.

EBR Principle

Understanding decays over time — unless the sender protects it from drift.

DAY 22 — The Drift Check as a Leadership Habit

The Lesson

If drift is communication's silent failure mode, then the **drift check** is its most effective countermeasure. A drift check is the simple, disciplined act of re-confirming shared understanding before assumptions accumulate into misalignment. It is not a meeting, a speech, or a reset — it is a habit. And like any habit, its power comes from consistency, not intensity. Leaders who practice drift checks don't wait for confusion to surface; they prevent it from forming.

A drift check is not re-explaining the original message. It is not repeating yourself. It is not a sign that people aren't smart or paying attention. It is a sign that you understand how human cognition works. Memory compresses. Context changes. Priorities shift. Interpretations drift. What was clear last week may not be clear today — and that is not a failure of the listener. It is a predictable feature of the human mind navigating a dynamic environment.

Great communicators normalize the drift check by making it part of their rhythm. They pause at key intervals and ask simple, alignment-building questions: *"What are we working from now?" "What assumptions have changed?" "What do we believe the priority is today?" "What has shifted since the last update?"* These questions bring tacit meaning back into the open. They expose small deviations while they are still cheap to correct. They stabilize the message before action drifts far enough to require repair.

The drift check also builds psychological safety. When leaders initiate recalibration, people no longer feel embarrassed to ask clarifying questions. They no longer assume they "should already know." They become more comfortable surfacing changes early instead of hiding uncertainty. Over time, teams develop a shared expectation: clarity will be maintained, not taken for granted. Alignment becomes a living state rather than a moment in time. The drift check turns communication from a one-time event into an ongoing process — one that holds its shape even as the environment evolves.

The Reflection

Think about a project, initiative, or daily routine that slowly became misaligned even though it started with shared clarity. What assumptions went unexamined? What quiet shifts in context or priority gradually altered the team's understanding? How much conflict or rework could have been avoided if you had paused for periodic drift checks instead of assuming the initial alignment would hold?

Now reflect on how often you revisit understanding with your team. Do you treat drift as an anomaly or as an expected force that requires routine attention? What would change in your leadership — and in your team's confidence — if drift checks became a normal part of how you maintain clarity?

The Commitment

- I will build drift checks into my leadership rhythm.
- I will surface small deviations before they grow into operational problems.
- I will normalize recalibration so clarity becomes a shared responsibility.
- I will treat drift checks as preventive control, not corrective cleanup.

EBR Principle

Clarity stays intact when leaders make drift checks a habit, not an exception.

DAY 23 — The Cost of Unchecked Drift

The Lesson

Drift is subtle when it begins, but expensive when it is ignored. Unchecked drift accumulates quietly in the gaps between intention and interpretation, and by the time the effects become visible, the organization is already paying for it. Tasks must be redone. Priorities conflict. Deadlines slip. People blame each other for outcomes they never agreed to. What started as a small difference in understanding grows into operational friction that steals time, erodes trust, and drains capacity. Drift is not just a communication issue — it is a cost center.

The most dangerous part of drift is that it masquerades as progress. People remain active, busy, and confident. They are still moving — just not together. The energy that should be pushing the team forward begins to work against itself. Two people solve the same problem separately. A team chases an outcome no longer aligned with current conditions. Someone continues applying yesterday's direction to today's situation. None of this dysfunction looks dramatic in the moment, but it compounds. Drift doesn't explode; it accumulates interest.

Unchecked drift also damages relationships. When people act from different versions of understanding, they interpret others' behavior through frustration rather than context. A delayed update looks like negligence. A misaligned decision looks like resistance. A misunderstood instruction looks like incompetence. Trust evaporates not because people are failing, but because their mental models are no longer synchronized. Communication becomes emotionally charged because clarity has decayed.

Great communicators treat drift as a financial, relational, and operational risk. They understand that every hour spent clarifying something that should have been maintained is an hour lost to rework. They understand that every misunderstanding allowed to grow becomes a credibility cost. They understand that alignment is cheaper to maintain than to rebuild. Preventing drift is not extra work — it is the work that prevents unnecessary work later.

The Reflection

Think about a time when a project, decision, or routine quietly drifted off course and no one noticed until the consequences appeared. How much effort went into repairing what drift had damaged? How much time was spent reconciling misunderstandings, resetting expectations, or redoing work that had already been done? What emotional or relational strain developed because people assumed the worst about each other instead of seeing the drift underneath?

Now consider how often you underestimate the cost of misalignment. What would change if you treated drift not as a communication inconvenience, but as an operational threat with real financial and human consequences?

The Commitment

- I will recognize drift as a source of cost, not just confusion.
- I will intervene early to prevent small misinterpretations from becoming expensive detours.
- I will reinforce alignment to protect time, trust, and team capacity.
- I will treat the prevention of drift as a strategic leadership responsibility.

EBR Principle

Drift is cheap to create but costly to ignore — prevention is the leader's advantage.

DAY 24 — Resetting Alignment After Drift

The Lesson

Even the best communication systems experience drift. No matter how clear the original message, interpretation shifts, context evolves, and people naturally reconstruct meaning over time. When drift is discovered, leaders face a critical choice: respond with frustration, or respond with alignment. The most effective communicators understand that reset moments are not signs of failure — they are opportunities to restore clarity, rebuild trust, and reaffirm shared direction. Resetting alignment is a skill, and the way it is handled determines whether the team recovers or fractures.

A reset is not a reprimand. It is not a moment to revisit blame or justify who "should have known better." Drift is predictable, and predictable phenomena should never be treated as personal shortcomings. When leaders express irritation during a reset, people become defensive, hide uncertainty, and drift accelerates underground. But when leaders treat drift as normal and correctable, psychological safety expands. People become more honest about what they understand, what they lost track of, and what needs realignment.

Resetting alignment requires three steps: **re-grounding the facts, re-stating the meaning, and re-establishing the path forward.** Re-grounding the facts resets the context: *Here's what's true now.* Re-stating the meaning re-centers interpretation: *Here's how we should understand the situation.* Re-establishing the path forward anchors action: *Here's what needs to happen next.* These steps repair understanding without shaming the listener or escalating tension. They close the gap between past assumptions and present reality.

Great communicators approach resets with steadiness, not judgment. They understand that drift is not a violation — it is a normal feature of human cognition. Resetting alignment is the work that keeps teams synchronized, relationships intact, and execution reliable. The reset is not a redo; it is a recalibration. It is leadership choosing clarity over frustration, alignment over ego, and forward momentum over dwelling on what drifted.

The Reflection

Think of a time when you discovered misalignment and felt frustrated because the message had already been explained. How did that emotional response affect the conversation? What assumptions did you make about why the drift occurred? Looking back, how might the reset have gone differently if you had approached it as a recalibration rather than a correction?

Now consider how your team responds when drift is uncovered. Do people become quiet, defensive, or hesitant? Or do they feel safe acknowledging what they lost track of? What would change in your environment if alignment resets were handled with steadiness, clarity, and zero blame?

The Commitment

- I will approach alignment resets as normal and necessary, not as failures.
- I will re-ground facts, re-state meaning, and re-establish clear next steps.
- I will remove blame from the reset process so people feel safe to recalibrate.
- I will treat resets as leadership opportunities to restore clarity and momentum.

EBR Principle

Drift is normal — resetting alignment is the leadership act that keeps teams unified.

DAY 25 — Cadence as a Control System

The Lesson

Communication does not stay aligned by accident. It stays aligned because leaders create a predictable **cadence** — a rhythm of touchpoints that stabilizes understanding before drift can take hold. Cadence is the control system of communication. It transforms clarity from something achieved occasionally into something maintained consistently. Without cadence, even strong communication degrades into fragmentation. With cadence, clarity becomes self-sustaining.

Cadence works because the human mind relies on rhythm. People remember what is reinforced. They stay aligned with what is revisited. They calibrate their interpretation to whatever is repeated, not whatever was said once. When leaders set a reliable cadence — daily huddles, weekly syncs, short check-ins, predictable updates — they are not adding meetings; they are creating the scaffolding that keeps meaning from collapsing under pressure and complexity. Cadence prevents people from drifting into separate timelines, separate priorities, and separate interpretations.

A healthy cadence is not about frequency — it is about **fit**. The rhythm must match the volatility, complexity, and interdependence of the work. High-tempo operations need fast cycles of communication; strategic initiatives need slower, deeper ones. Cadence must be right-sized: too sparse and drift expands, too heavy and clarity suffocates under noise. Great communicators design cadence intentionally, choosing the pace that keeps information fresh, expectations current, and interpretation synchronized.

Cadence also creates emotional stability. When people know when updates will occur, uncertainty shrinks. When they know when they can raise questions, stress decreases. When they know the next alignment point is coming, they stop jumping to conclusions. Cadence builds trust because it removes the unpredictability that fuels anxiety and overreaction. It signals reliability, discipline, and intentional leadership.

Ultimately, cadence is the system that keeps communication from becoming episodic. It ensures that clarity lives not only in the moment of explanation but in the ongoing rhythm that sustains understanding. Cadence turns communication from a series of events into a continuous operating process.

The Reflection

Think of a period when your team was overloaded, stretched, or moving quickly. How much of the confusion, rework, or frustration came from a lack of predictable communication rhythm? What decisions were made based on outdated assumptions simply because there was no structured moment to recalibrate? How much smoother would the work have been with a defined cadence anchoring everyone to the same version of reality?

Now reflect on your current leadership rhythm. Do your communication touchpoints match the pace and complexity of the work? Are people ever left waiting, guessing, or improvising because they don't know when clarity will return? What would change if cadence became intentional rather than reactive?

The Commitment

- I will design communication cadence to match the pace and complexity of the work.
- I will create predictable rhythms that keep interpretation aligned and current.
- I will use cadence to reduce uncertainty, prevent drift, and maintain shared focus.
- I will treat cadence as a control system — not an administrative task.

EBR Principle

Cadence keeps clarity alive — rhythm is the control system that prevents drift.

DAY 26 — Communication as a Reliability Process

The Lesson

Most organizations still treat communication as a social activity — something that happens through conversation, explanation, updates, or presentations. But high-performing teams view communication differently. They treat it as a **reliability process**, one that must produce consistent, predictable, and repeatable outcomes regardless of who delivers the message or when it is delivered. In this view, understanding becomes the product, alignment becomes the quality standard, and the leader becomes the process owner. Communication stops being casual and becomes engineered.

When communication is treated informally, results vary wildly. Two leaders deliver the same message and get two completely different outcomes. One team interprets instruction correctly; another drifts within hours. One shift aligns tightly; the next makes decisions based on outdated assumptions. These inconsistencies are not about intelligence or attitude — they are symptoms of an unreliable communication process. Without structure, variation becomes the norm. And in any system where variation grows, performance declines.

Great communicators remove this variation by redefining communication as a discipline rooted in reliability principles. They build communication paths that are standardized, clear, evidence-anchored, and verification-driven. They understand that if the process is sound, the product — shared understanding — becomes predictable. Just as equipment needs preventive maintenance, communication needs routine alignment checks, recalibration, and drift management. Just as operations rely on standard work, communication relies on structured sequencing. And just as systems require quality assurance, communication requires validation of interpretation before moving forward.

This shift changes everything. It reframes communication as a controllable, measurable part of leadership rather than an unpredictable art. It equips teams with a shared method for building meaning, reducing drift, and coordinating action. And it allows leaders to create environments where clarity holds under pressure, ambiguity shrinks, and alignment becomes the organizational default rather than a lucky outcome. When communication becomes a reliability process, performance stabilizes — because understanding stabilizes.

The Reflection

Think of a time when two groups received the same information but executed in completely different ways. How much of that divergence came from treating communication informally instead of as a structured process? What variation in understanding went unnoticed because the message wasn't verified or maintained? And how much energy was lost to clarification, correction, or recovery simply because the communication process itself wasn't reliable?

Now consider how your team experiences communication today. Is understanding predictable, or does it vary by sender, timing, and context? What would shift if you approached communication with the same rigor you expect from your operational systems — standardized, validated, and continuously maintained?

The Commitment

- I will treat communication as a reliability process, not a casual exchange.
- I will design communication paths that reduce variation and increase predictability.
- I will use structure and verification to stabilize understanding across roles and shifts.
- I will make alignment a measurable outcome, not an assumed byproduct.

EBR Principle

Reliable performance requires reliable communication — understanding must be engineered, not hoped for.

DAY 27 — Proportional Communication

The Lesson

Not every message requires the same depth, detail, frequency, or intensity. Yet many leaders communicate as if every situation should receive equal attention — or worse, they communicate inconsistently, giving major decisions a quick mention while over-explaining minor updates. High-reliability communication requires something more intentional: **proportional communication.** This principle states that the depth and frequency of communication must match a person's role, influence, risk exposure, and level of responsibility in the outcome. In other words, those who bear the most consequence must receive the most clarity.

Without proportionality, communication becomes either overwhelming or insufficient. Over-communication at the wrong level causes confusion, dilution, and noise. Under-communication where stakes are high produces drift, rework, and unnecessary risk. A senior leader may need context, implications, and strategic alignment; a front-line operator may need precise, evidence-backed direction. A cross-functional team may require broad visibility; a specialist may require technical detail. When leaders communicate without adjusting to these differences, the message becomes misaligned with the people who must act on it.

Great communicators calibrate their communication with intention. They ask: *Who is affected most? Who carries the greatest risk if this is misunderstood? Who needs full context? Who only needs the next step? Who needs to understand implications across teams? Who needs clarity on boundaries, not details?* Proportionality honors people's roles by giving them the level of information necessary to succeed — no more, no less. It respects their time, reduces noise, and increases accuracy.

When communication is proportional, alignment strengthens because the right people receive the right clarity at the right depth. Decisions improve because the people closest to the consequences are fully informed. Coordination improves because stakeholders share the context needed for synchronization.

Drift decreases because no one is forced to guess beyond their visibility. Proportional communication is not about doing less — it is about doing the **right** amount for the **right** people.

The Reflection

Think about a recent situation where someone acted incorrectly, not because they misunderstood, but because they never received the level of information appropriate for their role. Did you give too much detail to the wrong person? Too little detail to the right one? How did the imbalance affect execution, confidence, or coordination? What assumptions did you make about who needed what level of clarity?

Now consider your communication patterns. Do you default to one communication style for everyone, or do you tailor depth and frequency based on risk and responsibility? What would improve if your communication became intentionally proportional rather than evenly distributed?

The Commitment

- I will tailor communication depth and frequency to the role, not the moment.
- I will provide the greatest clarity to those with the greatest consequence.
- I will reduce noise by giving people the level of information they actually need.
- I will make proportionality a deliberate part of how I design communication.

EBR Principle

Clarity must match responsibility — communication is only effective when it is proportional.

DAY 28 — Communication as Collaboration

The Lesson

Most people think of communication as a transfer — information moving from one person to another. But high-reliability communication is not a transfer; it is a **collaboration**. Meaning is not delivered fully formed. It is co-constructed. Every message requires the listener to build understanding, surface assumptions, and apply context. When leaders treat communication as a one-way broadcast, they unintentionally shut down the very collaboration required to produce accurate interpretation. The result is a team that hears the words but never fully participates in the meaning.

Collaboration begins when leaders stop viewing their audience as passive receivers and start viewing them as active partners in constructing clarity. Instead of merely telling, they invite response. Instead of assuming alignment, they check it. Instead of protecting authority, they protect understanding. Communication becomes something created *with* people, not done *to* them. This shift is not soft — it is strategic. It recognizes that the listener carries half the responsibility for building meaning, and the leader carries the responsibility for engaging that half.

When communication becomes collaborative, people stop pretending they understand. They ask better questions. They reveal concerns early. They contribute context the leader may not see. Collaboration surfaces blind spots, aligns expectations, and strengthens ownership because people helped build the message, not just receive it. It transforms communication from compliance — "I'll do what you said" — into partnership — "We understand what this means, and we're moving together."

Great communicators cultivate this collaborative environment with deliberate behaviors. They pause for interpretation. They invite clarification. They ask how the message affects downstream work. They create space for disagreement before committing to action. They understand that every participant brings valuable information, and alignment requires pooling that insight rather than assuming the sender holds all of it. Communication becomes a shared construction of meaning — fast, accurate, and resilient under pressure.

The Reflection

Think about a time when you communicated clearly but later learned that someone had context you didn't know — context that would have changed the conversation if it had surfaced early. What opportunity for collaboration did you miss? How much rework or misalignment grew because the communication felt like a broadcast rather than an exchange?

Now consider your own patterns. How often do you pause to invite interpretation, questions, or alternative perspectives? How often do you treat communication as final instead of iterative? What would shift if you engaged people as partners in building meaning rather than passengers being informed?

The Commitment

- I will treat communication as a collaborative process, not a one-way transfer.
- I will invite interpretation, questions, and perspective to strengthen shared meaning.
- I will create space for people to contribute context I may not see.
- I will build alignment with people, not deliver it to them.

EBR Principle

Communication becomes reliable when it becomes collaborative — meaning is built together, not delivered alone.

DAY 29 — Surfacing Unintended Consequences Early

The Lesson

Every message, decision, and direction carries consequences — some intended, some predictable, and some that remain hidden until they disrupt the work. Communication becomes fragile when leaders assume the listener will naturally recognize these downstream effects on their own. In reality, people interpret messages through the lens of their immediate responsibilities, not the broader system. This makes **unintended consequences** one of the most common and costly byproducts of communication. The sooner they are surfaced, the sooner alignment can be protected.

Unintended consequences appear when people take correct actions that produce unexpected results. A shift supervisor reallocates labor, causing a backlog elsewhere. A team accelerates one priority, delaying another that depended on it. A well-meaning adjustment creates hidden risk downstream. None of these outcomes stem from incompetence; they stem from incomplete communication — communication that provided direction but not the visibility required to foresee ripple effects. People can't avoid consequences they can't see.

Great communicators actively surface unintended consequences early by creating space for reflection, challenge, and foresight before action accelerates. They ask questions that widen the listener's perspective: *"What might this affect that we haven't considered?" "Who else touches this?" "If this goes well, what changes downstream?" "If this goes wrong, where would we feel it first?"* These prompts expose assumptions, illuminate blind spots, and reveal friction points long before they turn into operational failures. Surfacing unintended consequences is not about predicting everything — it is about preventing preventable surprises.

When leaders embed this discipline into their communication, teams become more thoughtful, more anticipatory, and more connected. People stop acting in isolation because they learn to consider the broader system. Risk decreases because vulnerabilities appear before they activate. Alignment strengthens because decisions are made with full awareness of their impact. Surfacing unintended consequences is one of the most powerful ways to turn communication from reactive cleanup into proactive clarity.

The Reflection

Think of a moment when a well-intended decision created unexpected problems downstream. What information or perspective was missing that would have revealed the risk earlier? Who might have anticipated the consequence if they had been included or asked? How much time, stress, or rework resulted from a surprise that could have been surfaced with a simple question about downstream effects?

Now consider your communication habits. How often do you pause to ask about consequences before moving to action? How often do you rely on people to foresee impacts without helping them think systemically? What would shift if every important conversation included a moment to explore what could happen — not just what should happen?

The Commitment

- I will ask questions that surface unintended consequences before they appear.
- I will widen the frame of communication, so people see beyond their immediate role.
- I will involve those who can illuminate downstream impacts early.
- I will treat the prevention of unintended consequences as part of clarity, not luck.

EBR Principle

Unintended consequences shrink when leaders surface them early — before action amplifies them.

DAY 30 — The Complete EBR Alignment Loop

The Lesson

Every organization communicates, but few communicate in a way that produces consistent, repeatable alignment. Messages get delivered, but meaning drifts. Direction is given, but execution varies. Updates occur, but unintended consequences ripple through the system. The **EBR Alignment Loop** exists to solve this problem. It is the full, systematic cycle of communication that ensures understanding is built, verified, coordinated, and maintained over time: **Context (with Evidence) → Interpretation → Confirmation → Coordination → Drift Check.** When leaders follow this sequence, communication becomes reliable — not a gamble.

The loop begins with **Context and Evidence**, grounding the message in what is observable, real, and stable. Evidence prevents narrative-making, fear-based interpretation, and unnecessary assumptions. It gives the message a factual anchor. Next comes **Interpretation**, where leaders guide how the message should be understood. This step prevents meaning from forming in isolation or being shaped by stress, workload, or history. Most communication fails at this point because leaders skip the work of meaning-making.

The third step is **Confirmation**, the discipline of validating the meaning built in the listener's mind. This is where the sender inspects understanding, not assumes it. Confirmation replaces nods and politeness with clarity and alignment. Once meaning is shared, the loop moves to **Coordination**, transforming understanding into synchronized movement. Coordination names who needs to act, who needs to adjust, who depends on whom, and how the downstream system is affected. Without this step, aligned individuals still produce misaligned outcomes.

Finally comes the **Drift Check**, the maintenance step that preserves alignment over time. Even the best communication decays unless it is refreshed. Drift checks recalibrate understanding, expose shifting assumptions, and stabilize meaning before divergence becomes costly. The power of the EBR Alignment

Loop is not in any single step, but in the completeness of the cycle. When all five elements are present, communication becomes a process — predictable, durable, and resistant to drift. When even one step is missing, clarity becomes fragile.

The Reflection

Think back over the past month of communication challenges — the misunderstandings, the rework, the friction, the moments where effort exceeded results. Which parts of the loop were absent? Did you skip grounding in evidence? Did you fail to guide interpretation? Did you assume understanding instead of confirming it? Did you give direction without coordinating roles? Did you trust alignment to hold without checking for drift? How much of that pain could have been prevented with a complete communication loop rather than a partial one?

Now consider your leadership going forward. What would change if this loop became your default rhythm for every important message? How much clarity, speed, and cohesion would you recover simply by treating communication as a full-cycle system rather than a one-time event?

The Commitment

- I will follow the full EBR Alignment Loop instead of relying on partial communication.
- I will guide interpretation, confirm understanding, and coordinate action intentionally.
- I will use evidence and drift checks to stabilize clarity over time.
- I will treat communication as an engineered process that requires completeness, not convenience.

EBR Principle

Alignment is not a moment — it is a loop. Communication becomes reliable only when the entire cycle is followed.

BONUS DAY — Communication as a Leadership Identity

The Lesson

Across these thirty days, you have explored communication not as a soft skill, not as charisma, and not as a personality trait — but as a system, a discipline, and a responsibility. Yet beneath all the structures, tools, and habits lies a deeper truth: communication is not just something leaders *do*; it is something leaders *are*. It is an identity, a way of showing up, a way of engineering clarity in a world that naturally drifts toward confusion. When leaders embrace communication as part of who they are, consistency replaces improvisation and reliability replaces intention alone.

Leadership identity is revealed not in the moments when communication is easy, but in the moments when pressure rises. Under stress, people default to habit. If communication is merely a technique, it will collapse under strain. But if communication is part of the leader's identity — something they see as essential to their integrity, their effectiveness, and their stewardship — the habits hold. They anchor messages in evidence even when emotions run high. They guide interpretation rather than broadcast information. They check understanding instead of assuming alignment. They coordinate instead of command. They prevent drift rather than react to it.

Identity-level communication creates cultural gravity. People begin to model what they experience. They adopt the structure. They anticipate the verification. They absorb the calmness of drift resets, the discipline of proportionality, the steadiness of cadence. Over time, communication norms shift. Clarity becomes expected. Drift becomes noticeable. Misunderstanding becomes discussable. And alignment becomes the organization's default setting rather than its occasional achievement.

Seeing communication as a leadership identity reframes the work. It is no longer about technique; it is about stewardship. It is about ensuring that the people who depend on your clarity never have to guess. It is about engineering a culture where meaning is built intentionally rather than left to chance. And it is about understanding that leadership is ultimately an act of translation — turning complexity into shared understanding, turning direction into coordinated action, and turning uncertainty into reliability.

The Reflection

Think about the leaders who shaped you — the ones who created stability, clarity, and confidence in uncertain moments. What made their communication powerful? Was it their words, or the consistency behind them? How did their habits signal who they were, not just what they were saying? What part of their identity do you see reflected in your own leadership today?

Now consider how you want people to experience your communication. Do you want them to feel informed or anchored? Directed or coordinated? Updated or supported? How would your leadership change if you treated communication not as a task to complete, but as a defining expression of how you lead?

The Commitment

- I will integrate communication into my leadership identity, not treat it as a technique.
- I will communicate with the consistency, clarity, and reliability I want others to model.
- I will anchor my leadership in the disciplines that build understanding and alignment.
- I will lead in a way that makes clarity a cultural expectation, not an organizational luxury.

EBR Principle

Communication is not only a skill — it is a leadership identity that shapes every outcome.

The 10 Communication Failure Modes (and Their Countermeasures)

A diagnostic guide for leaders who want to engineer clarity rather than gamble on it.

1. Failure Mode: Evidence-Free Messaging

Mechanism: Messages are delivered using assumptions, emotion, urgency, or opinion instead of observable facts.

Effect: The listener fills gaps with personal stories, fear, or organizational folklore, creating drift and distortion immediately.

Countermeasure: Begin every important message with **Context + Evidence** to stabilize meaning.

EBR Reinforcement: *Evidence anchors interpretation.*

2. Failure Mode: Unguided Interpretation

Mechanism: The leader explains the situation but does not guide the meaning the listener should build.

Effect: Two people hear the same words but form different interpretations — both confident, both misaligned.

Countermeasure: Define the meaning explicitly: *"Here's how to understand this…"*

EBR Reinforcement: *Interpretation is the sender's responsibility.*

3. Failure Mode: Assumed Understanding

Mechanism: The leader mistakes nods, agreement, or silence as evidence of comprehension.

Effect: The listener walks away certain but incorrect; misalignment surfaces only when consequences occur.

Countermeasure: Use verification: *"Tell me how you're interpreting this."*

EBR Reinforcement: *Understanding must be confirmed, not inferred.*

4. Failure Mode: Missing Implications

Mechanism: Direction is given without naming downstream effects, dependencies, or impacts.

Effect: People make reasonable decisions that collide with others' work, causing friction, rework, and delay.

Countermeasure: Clarify implications before action: *"Here's what this changes…"*

EBR Reinforcement: *Clarity must extend downstream.*

5. Failure Mode: Action-Free Messages

Mechanism: Communication ends in awareness, not direction.

Effect: People agree with the message but act inconsistently because next steps were never stated.

Countermeasure: End every message with the precise required action — no exceptions.

EBR Reinforcement: *Clarity becomes real only when it becomes action.*

6. Failure Mode: Isolated Communication

Mechanism: Information is given to individuals without visibility into who else knows or how work intersects.

Effect: People make isolated decisions that unintentionally disrupt others.

Countermeasure: Widen the frame — name who's involved, who's affected, and who must coordinate.

EBR Reinforcement: *Communication succeeds when it prevents isolation.*

7. Failure Mode: Filter-Blind Messaging

Mechanism: The leader communicates from their own perspective, ignoring the listener's workload, fears, incentives, and experiences.

Effect: Messages distort instantly, reconstructed through stress, bias, or history.

Countermeasure: Design messaging for the **receiver's filters**, not the sender's mindset.

EBR Reinforcement: *Meaning forms inside their world, not yours.*

8. Failure Mode: Drift Accumulation

Mechanism: Meaning decays over time because the leader assumes understanding remains stable.

Effect: Team members operate on old interpretations while conditions evolve.

Countermeasure: Implement routine **drift checks** — recalibrate before deviation grows.

EBR Reinforcement: *Understanding decays unless maintained.*

9. Failure Mode: Unsurfaced Consequences

Mechanism: The leader communicates direction but never asks what might go wrong or where surprises could appear.

Effect: Unintended consequences emerge later, costing time, trust, and energy.

Countermeasure: Surface consequences early: *"What might this affect?"*

EBR Reinforcement: *Early insight prevents late crisis.*

10. Failure Mode: Partial Alignment Loop

Mechanism: The leader uses some steps of the EBR Alignment Loop but ignores others — often skipping confirmation or coordination.

Effect: Messages begin clear but end inconsistent, because the process was incomplete.

Countermeasure: Follow the full loop: **Context → Interpretation → Confirmation → Coordination → Drift Check.**

EBR Reinforcement: *Alignment is a loop, not an event.*

The EBR Communication Scripts for Tough Moments

Pre-engineered language for moments where clarity matters most.

1. Resetting Drift

Purpose: Recalibrate understanding without blame.

The Script:
"Let's reset together. Here's what's true right now, here's how we should understand it, and here's what needs to happen next. If anything has shifted since we last talked, let's surface it so we're working from the same picture."

Why This Works:
It follows the drift-reset sequence—facts, meaning, next steps—without assigning fault, preserving psychological safety and restoring alignment.

2. Correcting Misinterpretation

Purpose: Realign meaning when someone built a reasonable but incorrect interpretation.

The Script:
"Let me clarify how this should be understood. I can see how you got to your interpretation, but here's the meaning we need to work from. The part that needs correction is ____. Here's the updated understanding moving forward."

Why This Works:
It validates the other person's reasoning (reducing defensiveness), then replaces the inaccurate meaning with the intended one.

3. Asking for Confirmation ("Show Me Your Interpretation")

Purpose: Verify understanding before action.

The Script:
"Before we move forward, tell me how you're interpreting this. I want to make sure we're working from the same meaning and not from different assumptions."

Why This Works:
It signals that verification is normal and expected, not a test. It uncovers gaps early—before they turn into misalignment.

4. Stopping Unilateral Decision-Making

Purpose: Prevent someone from acting in isolation and creating downstream friction.

The Script:
"Pause for a moment. This decision affects more than your area alone. Before we move forward, let's pull in the people downstream so we don't create unintended consequences. Here's who we need to loop in and why."

Why This Works:
It redirects the moment without blame and reinforces coordination as a norm, not a courtesy.

5. Communicating Up (to Senior Leaders)

Purpose: Provide clarity, not noise; surface risk without drama.

The Script:
"Here's the current situation, here's the evidence we're working from, and here's the implication if nothing changes. The decision point I need from you is ____. If we choose option A, here's the downstream impact. If we choose option B, here's the impact. My recommendation is ____ based on the evidence."

Why This Works:
Leaders want evidence, implications, and a decision request—not narration. This script matches their cognitive rhythm.

6. Communicating Down (to Frontline Teams)

Purpose: Remove ambiguity and guide interpretation clearly.

The Script:
"Here's what's happening, here's what it means for us, and here's the action we need to take. If anything in this doesn't match what you're seeing on the floor, speak up so we can align fast."

Why This Works:
Frontline work requires clarity and relevance. This script makes meaning explicit and invites real-world correction.

7. Communicating Across (Peer-to-Peer)

Purpose: Avoid territorial assumptions and coordinate shared responsibilities.

The Script:
"Here's the update from my side, here's how it affects your area, and here's where our work overlaps. Before either of us adjusts anything, let's agree on the shared picture so we don't create cross-pressure."

Why This Works:
Peers often drift fastest. This script establishes shared visibility and prevents quiet misalignment.

8. Delivering Early, Difficult Information

Purpose: Communicate truth early to stabilize interpretation and reduce anxiety.

The Script:
"I want to get this to you early so we're not interpreting it through rumor or urgency. Here's what we know, here's what we don't know yet, and here's how we're going to move forward while we learn more."

Why This Works:
It prevents fear-based meaning-making by pairing early communication with transparency about uncertainty.

9. Stopping a Meeting That's Drifting

Purpose: Re-anchor the conversation before it derails into confusion or circular debate.

The Script:
"Let's pause and reset. Here's the original purpose, here's where we are now, and here's what we need to decide before we move on. If something changed that we haven't acknowledged, let's surface it."

Why This Works:
It prevents wasted time and realigns the group around purpose without calling anyone out individually.

10. Addressing a Pattern of Miscommunication

Purpose: Correct recurring issues without shame or accusation.

The Script:
"I've noticed we're interpreting messages differently more often than we'd expect. That tells me the communication process needs tightening, not that anyone is failing. Let's walk through how we're each making meaning so we can eliminate the drift."

Why This Works:
It reframes the issue as a *process* problem, not a *person* problem—preserving relationships while improving alignment.

Communication – A 30-Day Mindsets Transformation Guide

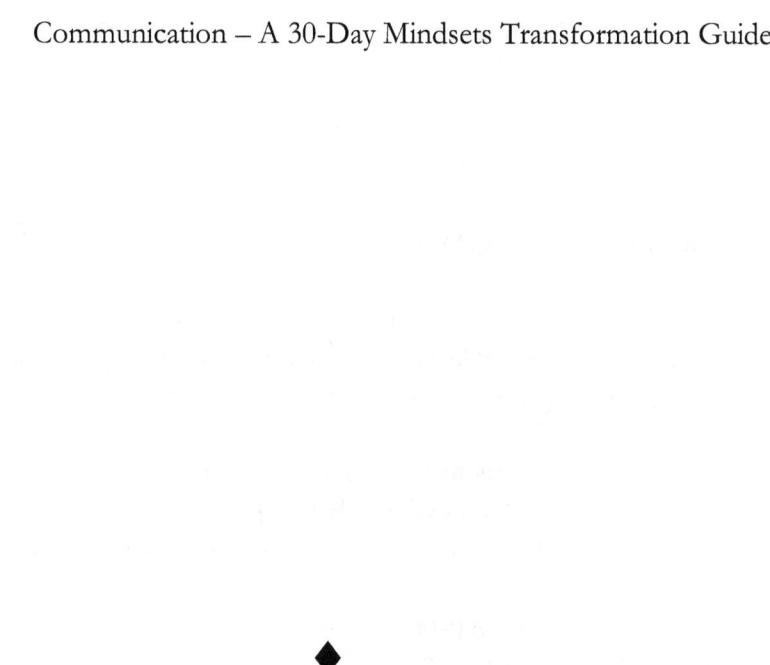

The Proportional Communication Map

("Who Needs What and When")

The Proportional Communication Map is the operational tool that turns the Proportionality Principle into day-to-day practice. It helps a leader answer the three essential questions of responsible communication:

1. **Who actually needs this information?**
2. **What level of detail do they require?**
3. **When do they need it to operate effectively and without surprises?**

Instead of categorizing people by hierarchy, title, or the overused term you asked me to avoid, the map organizes communication by **functional dependency**.

In other words:

Who is affected by the work, the decision, or the outcome — and in what way?

The Four Functional Groups

The map divides your environment into four distinct groups, each defined by how the work flows, how decisions propagate, and how consequences travel:

1. The Contributors

These are the people whose work directly builds, executes, maintains, or performs the activity.
They need **the highest level of clarity, earliest notice, and the greatest depth**, because their execution determines whether the action succeeds.

What they need:
— Clear expectations
— Exact sequence of next steps
— Timing, constraints, and criteria for success
— Immediate updates whenever conditions change

When they need it:
Before movement, before change, and always before risk arrives.

2. The Coordinators

These are the people whose work must align with your work so neither group causes friction, drift, or rework for the other. Their performance is indirectly dependent on the clarity of your communication, even though they don't execute your tasks themselves.

What they need:
— Early visibility
— Dependencies and impacts
— Changes that affect timing, handoffs, or resource load

When they need it:
As soon as decisions are made and before any schedule, resource, or workflow conflict becomes real.

3. The Consumers

These are the people who will use, rely on, or be affected by the output of the work. They aren't performing the task, and they don't coordinate it — but their world changes because of it.

What they need:
— What is changing
— What it means for them
— What they must do differently
— Timing of when the output becomes available or valid

When they need it:
Before the product, update, or consequence touches them.

4. The Observers

These individuals don't execute, coordinate, or consume the work, but they benefit from awareness: leaders, support roles, or peripheral functions who must maintain situational understanding.

What they need:
— High-level updates
— Major changes
— Confirmation that progress is occurring

When they need it:
Periodically; usually on milestones or at decision gates.

How to Use the Map

For any decision, update, change, or event, walk through the four questions:

1. **Who are the Contributors?**
2. **Who are the Coordinators?**
3. **Who are the Consumers?**
4. **Who are the Observers?**

Then determine, for each group:

- What they must understand
- What action is expected of them
- What timing ensures they are never surprised
- What level of detail is proportional to their role

This allows you to **engineer communication in layers**, proportional to impact and responsibility.

Why It Works

Because it aligns perfectly with your framework:

- **Responsibility is on the Sender** to engineer understanding.
- **Interpretation must be designed**, not assumed.
- **Validation is mandatory**, not optional.
- **No one gets information late**, and no one gets more than they need.
- **Communication becomes operationally tied** to flow of work, not personal preference or politics.

This map becomes the leader's internal compass for "who needs what and when," turning communication into a predictable, repeatable discipline — one that prevents drift, over-communication, under-communication, and the costly surprises that follow.

The EBR Communication Audit Tool

A Structured Checklist to Evaluate the Quality and Reliability of a Communication Event

The EBR Communication Audit Tool is a disciplined, post-event checklist that determines whether a communication actually *worked*. It evaluates whether the sender engineered clarity, confirmed interpretation, and removed uncertainty — or whether gaps, drift, or ambiguity were allowed to form.

This tool is not a survey. It is not a "how did it feel?" questionnaire.

It is a **reliability assessment for communication:**

Did understanding transfer? Did alignment hold? Did the message produce the intended action without confusion, delay, or rework?

The audit is divided into five categories that map directly to the EBR Communication Framework. Each category contains objective yes/no items that force the evaluator to judge communication not by intent but by outcome.

1. Clarity and Construction of the Message

- ☐ The message clearly stated **what was happening, why,** and **what it meant.**
- ☐ The message avoided abstraction, implication, and vague directional language.
- ☐ The sender used evidence, not assumptions, as the foundation.
- ☐ The sender pre-built the interpretation by providing the necessary context.
- ☐ No part of the message required the listener to "figure it out."

2. Design for Interpretation

- ☐ The sender anticipated likely misinterpretations and addressed them directly.
- ☐ The message was sequenced logically: evidence → interpretation → implication → required action.
- ☐ The sender reduced ambiguity by naming constraints, risks, and required decisions.
- ☐ The communication accounted for workload, incentives, past history, and emotional filters.
- ☐ No reliance on "they'll get it" or "they know what I mean."

3. Verification and Confirmation

- ☐ The sender actively checked for comprehension, not agreement.
- ☐ The listener was asked to restate their understanding in their own words.
- ☐ The sender validated both the **interpretation** and the **intended next action**.
- ☐ The communication included a check-for-drift prompt ("What could cause this to go off track?").
- ☐ Silence or nods were *not* accepted as confirmation.

4. Timing and Proportionality

- ☐ Communication occurred *before* any irreversible movement, decision, or risk.
- ☐ Updates were delivered early — not after consequences were already in motion.
- ☐ The sender delivered only the amount of information proportional to each group's role.
- ☐ People who depended on the message received it exactly when they needed it — not later.
- ☐ No one received more detail than required to act successfully.

5. Outcome Reliability

- ☐ The listener walked away knowing exactly what to think and what to do next.
- ☐ No rework, confusion, or clarifying follow-up was required later.
- ☐ Downstream handoffs occurred smoothly and without contradictions.
- ☐ No unexpected consequences resulted from misunderstood information.
- ☐ The communication preserved alignment — no drift occurred over time.

How to Score the Audit

- **18–25 "Yes" answers:**
  High-reliability communication. The event met EBR standards.
- **10–17 "Yes" answers:**
  Moderate reliability. Some success, but drift and re-explanation are likely.
- **0–9 "Yes" answers:**
  Low reliability. The communication depended on luck rather than design.

How to Use This Tool in Real Time

- Use it **post-meeting** to diagnose where clarity broke.
- Use it **pre-meeting** as a preparation checklist.
- Use it **after every failed communication** to pinpoint root causes.
- Use it **as a team standard**, teaching others how communication must be engineered, not improvised.

This audit becomes the organization's quality check — the equivalent of a torque wrench for communication.
It ensures that what was said is actually what was understood, and that what was understood is actually what gets done.

Communication – A 30-Day Mindsets Transformation Guide

The EBR Conversation Builder Template

A Fill-in-the-Blank Guide for Preparing High-Stakes Conversations**

High-stakes conversations fail for one core reason: the sender *hopes* clarity will happen instead of *engineering* it.
The EBR Conversation Builder Template removes the improvisation and forces the communicator to construct the message with precision, intentionality, and verification.

This template is built on the EBR sequence:

Evidence → Interpretation → Implication → Required Action → Confirmation

When completed, it becomes a ready-to-deliver script that ensures the conversation produces alignment instead of drift.

Step 1: Define the Evidence (What Is Observable and True)

The facts the listener must understand first:

- "The current situation is: _____."
- "Here is what we know for certain: _____."
- "Here is the data/observation/event that triggered this conversation: _____."

Avoid opinions, motives, predictions, or narrative. Only observable signal.

Step 2: Build the Interpretation (What the Evidence Actually Means)

The meaning the sender must construct, not leave to chance:

- "What this means is: _____."
- "The key point I need you to take from this is: _____."
- "Here is the correct way to understand this situation: _____."

This prevents the listener from generating their own (incorrect) interpretation.

Step 3: State the Implication (What Changes Because of This)

The consequence, impact, or operational meaning:

- "Because of this, here is what changes: _____."
- "Here is what becomes possible / impossible / risky: _____."
- "Here is what this means for our timeline, resources, or priorities: _____."

This step connects understanding to reality — removing ambiguity.

Step 4: Define the Required Action (What Must Happen Next)

Tell the listener exactly what to do, not simply what to think:

- "Here is what needs to happen next: _____."
- "Your role is to: _____."
- "The deliverable or outcome I need from you is: _____."
- "The timing / sequence we must follow is: _____."

Action is where communication becomes operational.

Step 5: Confirm Understanding (Do Not Assume — Verify)

Ask the listener to restate the message back using their own words:

- "Tell me how you're interpreting this."
- "Walk me through your understanding of what needs to happen next."
- "Where do you see risk or potential drift?"
- "What part of this could be misunderstood if we don't tighten it up now?"

This is the sender's quality-control step — alignment is engineered, not inferred.

Optional: Anticipate Likely Drift Points

(To prevent misinterpretation before it happens)

- "The part people usually misunderstand here is: _____."
- "The risk I want to eliminate now is: _____."
- "If conditions change, the first thing you should communicate is: _____."

Optional: Set the Update Cadence

(To keep alignment from decaying over time)

- "Here is how often we will communicate updates_____."
- "Notify me immediately if: _____."
- "We will reconfirm alignment at: _____."

The Template in Practice

Leaders use this tool when:

- delivering difficult news
- assigning critical work
- correcting misinterpretation
- setting new expectations
- announcing changes
- realigning commitments
- briefing up or down the chain
- preventing future drift

Every high-stakes conversation becomes structured, predictable, and reliable.

Communication – A 30-Day Mindsets Transformation Guide

◆
―――――――――――――――――――――
◆

Closing Reflections

In the end, communication is not a soft skill — it is a structural responsibility. It is the discipline of transferring understanding with such clarity that drift has nowhere to hide. It is the craft of reducing uncertainty so people can act with confidence. It is the leadership behavior that determines whether a team moves in alignment or in fragments.

The lessons throughout this book pull you toward a single, unavoidable truth: **communication succeeds only when the sender chooses to engineer it.** Not improvise it. Not hope for it. Not rely on the receiver to interpret it or 'do their part'. But deliberately design it — with evidence, with sequence, with proportionality, and with verification.

Great communicators are not great because they talk well.
They are great because they **think clearly, prepare intentionally, and validate relentlessly.**
They know that comprehension is not a courtesy — it is an obligation.
They understand that silence is not alignment — it is ambiguity.
They recognize that most problems begin not with decisions, but with assumptions made in the absence of clarity.

As you apply these principles in your daily conversations, your updates, your briefings, and your leadership moments, you will notice something subtle: the room calms. Friction drops. People stop guessing. Work moves with fewer surprises. And trust strengthens — not because you are agreeable, but because you are reliable.

This is the quiet power of engineered communication:

- **It makes everyone's world easier.**
- It lets people think instead of react.
- It removes fear and replaces it with understanding.
- It builds a culture that can move fast because it moves together.

And in that space — the space where clarity replaces confusion — your leadership becomes visible. Consistency becomes your credibility. And evidence becomes the language people learn to rely on.

Carry these principles forward.
Return to them often.
Use them to build the moments that matter — because in the end, the quality of your communication becomes the quality of your leadership.

About the Author

Andy E. Page, Jr., Ph.D.

Founder, **EBR Technologies**
Creator of the **Evidence-Based Reliability (EBR)™ and RCM-FX™** frameworks

Andy Page is a reliability engineer, strategist, and educator who has spent more than two decades helping industrial organizations transform the way they think about maintenance, performance, and culture. His work bridges two worlds — the precision of data and the discipline of leadership.

As the founder of **EBR Technologies**, Andy developed the Evidence-Based Reliability (EBR) framework, a practical approach that helps teams replace emotion with evidence and chaos with control. His **RCM-FX** method redefines classical reliability-centered maintenance with deeper categorization of failure effects, layered protection logic, and a culture-first mindset that connects the shop floor to the boardroom.

Over his career, Andy has guided clients across manufacturing, utilities, energy, and consumer goods — helping leaders and technicians alike build systems that think before they break. His teaching style combines technical clarity with cultural insight, making reliability not just a technical function, but a leadership behavior.

When he's not writing or consulting, Andy speaks to global audiences about the intersection of foresight, data, and discipline — and how evidence can become the most trusted voice in an organization.

About EBR Technologies

EBR Technologies (Evidence-Based Reliability) is a reliability consulting and training organization focused on helping clients build systems that think, plan, and act with discipline.

Founded on the belief that reliability isn't assumed — it's engineered, EBR Technologies equips organizations with tools and frameworks to:
- Engineer foresight through structured analysis and evidence-driven planning.
- Strengthen execution through Work Execution Management (WEM) systems that eliminate friction.
- **S**hape culture through the R^3/R^4 Model — aligning what leaders Require, Reward, and Reinforce with what the organization's Rituals, Rhetoric, Role Models, and Routines display.

EBR's work spans reliability improvement roadmaps, criticality analysis, PM optimization, asset walkdowns, and full-scale cultural alignment programs designed to make evidence the language of leadership.

EBR Technologies
Evidence is our authority.

www.ebrtechnologies.com
info@ebrtechnologies.com

Author's Note on the Use of AI

This book was written in collaboration with an artificial intelligence tool — not as a shortcut, but as a companion in reflection.

Every lesson, mindset, and maxim within these pages originates from my years of teaching, consulting, and field experience in safety, reliability, and culture. The principles draw from my established models — the R3/R4 Culture Framework, the Evidence-Based Thinking philosophy, and the broader discipline of Leadership Alignment that I've practiced and refined across industries and organizations.

AI served here as an instrument, not an author. Like a disciplined editor with infinite patience, it helped shape language, surface clarity, and maintain consistency across hundreds of pages. But the thoughts, logic, and voice are entirely my own. Each reflection began with lived experience — moments in real plants, real teams, and real failures that taught what alignment truly means.

The machine assisted in structure; the meaning came from the field. It allowed me to capture ideas at the speed they occurred, to test phrasing against the very principles this book teaches — precision, coherence, and intent. The goal was never to let technology think for me, but to let it think with me, mirroring the process of inquiry that defines evidence-based leadership itself.

Every page has been reviewed, edited, and approved by me to ensure it aligns with the purpose of this work. The message is unchanged, whether typed by hand or accelerated by algorithm.

This book stands as proof that technology, when guided by experience and anchored by purpose, can amplify clarity without diluting conviction. The thinking remains human. The evidence remains real. The alignment remains intentional.

— *Andy Page Ph.D.*

www.ingramcontent.com/pod-product-compliance
Lightning Source LLC
Chambersburg PA
CBHW070204100426
42743CB00013B/3039